Tracing the Golden Thread

Mary Weeks Millard

Onwards and Upwards Publishers

Berkeley House,
11 Nightingale Crescent,
Leatherhead,
Surrey,
KT24 6PD.

www.onwardsandupwards.org

ISBN: 978-1-907509-49-0
Cover design: Guilherme Gustavo Condeixa

NOTE: Some of the names of patients and clients have been changed to protect their identity.

Dedication

I dedicate this book to all my nursing colleagues through the years, but especially to Joy, Jeannette, Heather and Margaret, who not only shared 'The Nursery' but have stayed my loyal friends through the years.

If I could live my life again,
I still would be a nurse;
Put on my cap and apron,
for better or for worse.

(Author unknown)

Contents

1

Early Years

I was never a child who played 'hospitals' with my dolls. Indeed, I can only ever remember owning two dolls when I was a girl. The first was a beautiful china doll, which I called Beryl after the half-cousin who had given it to me. She was already grown up when I was born and must have treasured her doll because it was almost like new when I received it. I can still visualise Beryl's blonde curly hair and bright blue eyes, set in the beautiful china face. How I loved that doll! Sadly, she was my treasured possession for just a few months before being smashed by my brother!

My second doll was given to me by my parents for my seventh birthday. This one was a 'baby' doll, decked in pretty, hand-knitted garments which my mother had lovingly made. I think it was to prepare me for the coming of another baby into our family three months later. This doll was only ever called Baby and was a wonderful present as toys were hard to come by after the end of the Second World War. Friends of the family who lived near our home had made a cot for my birthday doll, and it came with mattress, sheets and a pillow! Then my aunt gave me a patchwork quilt. I was the proudest little 'mother' in the world! This doll was made of a plastic type of material so could not be broken by my big or small brothers!

When my baby brother made his appearance a few months later, I had my first acquaintance with a nurse. Her name was Nurse Southgate, and she was the district midwife for the area. To me, she seemed rather old and forbidding, and I was not a little scared when she came to the door in her navy coat and hat with an embroidered badge on the band. In those days, it was quite normal to have a home birth, and the midwife attended every day for the ten day lying-in period. My brother, Timothy, had been born during the August school holidays so I was around when Nurse Southgate called. She must have 'taken a shine' to me because sometimes I was allowed to accompany her on her rounds, sitting beside her in her black car! I had hardly ever been in a car so it was a great adventure! I grew to like Nurse Southgate but was very much in awe of her. I learned much later that I owed my own life, humanly speaking, to her devotion and care. I had been born very, very prematurely and no one had believed that I would survive except this remarkable midwife; with great determination she had fed me milk and brandy through an eye dropper for several weeks until I was strong enough to suck! It was she who had weighed me for the first time when I was six weeks old. Even wrapped in clothes and a shawl I just tipped the scales at four pounds!

I never for one moment ever dreamt that one day I too would be a nurse and a midwife!

Life changed dramatically for me just before my tenth birthday. Our family moved from the tiny bungalow in Weymouth to what seemed to us, a very grand 'semi' in Bath! The best thing about the move was that, at last, we were able to live together as a family. For years Dad had been working near Bath coming home only at weekends. He had become a fairly shadowy figure in my life as much of the weekend he spent in church activities; he certainly had no time to play with his three children. Now we saw him every day! Once we were settled he brought his widowed mother to live near us, and this was another delight. Our grandmother was gentle and quiet, and I loved to spend time with her. I remember her reading stories to me even though she had only received a very elementary education.

I found it hard to make friends in my new school and dreaded going. It was the Girls and Infants Church School. My brother had to make his way over the river to the Boys School but only for a very short time as he soon transferred to the grammar school. My class teacher thought I was stupid, and the more she scolded me, the more tongue-tied I became. 'Spelling Bees' and Mental Arithmetic were my worst nightmare! How often I was called to the front and my knuckles rapped with the ruler! I began to believe that, indeed, I must be mentally deficient and very stupid. It didn't help that every lunch time I was made to go to the infants' room after lunch and rest on a little bed alongside them, having no option but to listen to all the little fairy stories which were being read to them! I was very small for my age and deemed not to be very strong, so was not allowed out to play with my classmates. I found myself increasingly isolated and lonely.

When it was time for our class to take the Eleven Plus selection test, I was duly sent home with a form for my parents to fill in. They had to select the schools they preferred. To me, it was a question of which secondary modern school they would choose, for my teacher had told me in no uncertain terms that I would never pass for the grammar school.

My father had different ideas! At the top of the list was a girls' public school which granted eight scholarships each year - four to pupils from the city of Bath and four to Somerset county schools. My father put that school as his first choice, followed by the grammar school, and ignoring the selection of a secondary modern school. I duly took the form back to school. The class teacher and the head mistress laughed together when they saw my father's selection and invited him to meet with them to discuss what they saw as my realistic future!

My father, a quiet and gentle man, looked at these formidable ladies and told them that the form would be submitted with the schools he had chosen for me. They tried to reason with him, then in exasperation told him that I was a 'backward' child and that if he wanted me to go to a public school then he had better be prepared to spend a lot of money on fees; they were sure I could not pass any entrance exam that would be required!

Along with all my class, I sat the Eleven Plus exam. I do not remember it causing me any anxiety or stress. I just got on with it, and life went on. Eventually, before the results arrived, my parents received a letter inviting me for an interview at the public school! I think, perhaps, that even they were astounded. My mother set to work and smocked me a red-

and-white striped dress. At least she would make sure that I would look smartly dressed at the interview! My class teacher, on hearing the news, was equally astounded and from then on treated me a little more kindly. She even sent me to the headmistress, who gave me a mock interview. I was very shy and withdrawn, quite unable to answer her questions.

The day of the interview arrived, and my mother duly escorted me to the High School. We waited in a beautiful hall, in what must once have been an exquisite mansion. I remember gazing up at the ceiling, then down at the marble floor. Sometimes girls walked past us, neat in their uniforms and seeming very grown up to me. Our turn arrived, and my mother and I were ushered into the headmistress' office. She was a middle-aged lady with a kind smile. At first she asked my mother a lot of questions, and I began to relax. Maybe she wouldn't ask me anything, and I wouldn't have to do Mental Arithmetic or spell words out loud!

Then she asked my mother to wait outside. My anxiety increased, and my mouth went dry; panic rose within me! With a smile on her face she handed me a book and asked me to read a poem about the sea. I was in my element! I forgot I was being interviewed as I lost myself in the beauty of the words and felt transported back to the seaside town where we had lived. I could see the harbour and smell the sea! I was able to answer the head's questions without hesitation. Something flashed in my mind that I was not completely stupid!

Then the head complimented me on my pretty dress! I was a very plain child, and money had been very tight in the post-war period so I was not used to such compliments. I proudly explained that my mother had made it for me!

Whether it was due to the poem about the sea or my mother's dressmaking I shall never know, but I was given one of the four scholarships granted to Bath girls!

Suddenly everything changed at my primary school! Instead of being the dunce, I was now a celebrity! No-one in the history of the school had ever gained a place at the Bath High School for Girls!! However, I still felt isolated because no-one else from the school or even the neighbourhood would be going with me to the new school.

Looking back, I see God's almighty hand and his humour in my transfer to senior school. We are told that he has "plans for us to give us a hope and a future." (Jeremiah 29 v.11) He had chosen a career for me and a life path and opened the way to prepare me for it.

Senior School and Beyond

These days children are transported to school in various ways and the new entrants to senior school are normally admitted a day before the term starts so that they can be shown around the complex and meet their teachers. There were no such luxuries in my day!

My first day at senior school, dressed in my new uniform, with a satchel on my back, I walked the two miles (mostly uphill) on my own and nervously entered the building. The first two years' groups of the senior section of the school were housed in a separate building, which did make life a little easier for us. Many of the girls were very much at ease for they had been in the junior school. Some were boarders and had already settled in and made friends. Those of us who were new entrants were surprisingly few, but we too began to make friends and settle down. For me, one hurdle was to begin to learn French. Many of the other pupils had already been taught the language for a couple of years, but for me it was a completely new subject. I didn't find it as hard as I had feared and at the end of the first term was promoted from second to first division. I was elated by that! Once again, looking back, I can see God's hand in this because it gave me a love for the language and confidence that I could learn it. Little did I ever guess that one day I would need to not only speak but also teach in French in the Congo!

As my confidence grew, I began to enjoy school. I tried to do my best and even enjoyed homework! My parents were encouraging and always gave me time to study even though there were many jobs which I was expected to do to help at home. My mother was going blind and needed help, especially with caring for my small brother. I loved him dearly, and pushed him out most Saturdays. During my second term at the senior school he caught mumps. It must have been a really bad infection because Tim became delirious one night, and I sat up with him. This was my first attempt at nursing! In the morning the doctor was called. I presume that it was a Saturday because I was home from school. Having examined my little brother, the doctor then addressed my mother.

"Can I look at Mary's spine?" he asked her.

Mother was a bit mystified.

"Why?" she asked. "What is wrong?"

"I can see that she is developing a slight hump," he answered. "It may be nothing, but it would be good to check it."

By this time I was becoming embarrassed! I was a growing girl, nearing twelve years old, and did not want to strip off in the dining room in front of everyone! However, the doctor was held in high esteem, and so strip off I did, my face as red as a beetroot!

"Hump!" the doctor grunted. "Do you get backache, Mary?"

"Some," I muttered.

I had lived with backache so long that it seemed normal to me. Certainly it had become worse since learning to play hockey and doing more physical exercise in the gymnasium at school. Carrying my satchel home after school, full of books, also made it ache.

"I think we should send Mary to see a consultant at the Bath and Wessex Orthopaedic Hospital," the doctor announced to my surprised mother. "Her spine has a curvature. We must find out why."

So began a long period of hospitalisation. I was experiencing nursing first hand! Most of the nurses were very young, doing two years' training in orthopaedics before they began their general training. They looked so smart in their striped dresses, starched aprons and pleated caps! They were very kind and friendly to us all.

The hospital was for children. There was a mixed ward for babies and toddlers, then a girls' ward and a boys' ward. I don't ever remember seeing a boy so we must have been kept well apart!

Some children came for short periods, but most of us came for months! Many children had been sent from far flung corners of Britain, as the hospital was a centre of excellence and used the hot mineral springs for treatments. We had a school, of sorts, but it did not meet my needs very well, and so my parents collected work from my school and brought it in, hoping I wouldn't fall too far behind. In spite of this, I did worry that I wouldn't be able to manage when I went back and was so afraid of becoming (as I thought) 'stupid' again.

Life was very austere in the hospital. Parents were allowed to visit, but visiting times were infrequent and short. The rules were rigidly observed. My family lived less than a mile down the road, but some girls hardly ever saw their families. I shall never forget one young girl, maybe about eight or ten years old, called Janice. She had rheumatoid arthritis, and her limbs had severe contractures. Both arms and legs were hung in slings, and she had so much pain when she was moved - but she rarely moaned or complained. She was never allowed out of bed. Her family lived in Lancashire, and I do not remember them visiting through the months I was in the ward.

On Monday evenings, two ladies came to the ward and ran what was called 'Sunday Monday School'. We called the ladies 'Auntie Edna' and 'Auntie Joan'. Monday evenings became the highlight of the week for us! I can even remember one of the talks, sixty years on! Auntie Edna showed us her birth certificate. I am not sure if I had ever seen one before. She explained how it showed she had been born in England and was a citizen here. Then she explained how we needed to have our names written in God's book of life, to be born into his family and be citizens of heaven. I didn't do anything about it at that stage, but the words went deep into my heart.

We were allowed to choose our favourite choruses to sing, and little Janice always chose 'Count your blessings; name them one by one'! That also made a deep impression on me; for of all of us on the ward, it seemed to me that she had the most to grumble about.

I certainly grumbled!

I hated the food in that hospital! Most of all I hated it being served on tin plates and mugs! Every evening we had thin soup and dry bread. It made me feel sick! Even as I think about it, I can almost smell it again! I used to beg my mum to bring in her lovely homemade cakes and sweets! When she did, they were taken by the sister and shared out to everyone. I never minded too much about that because I felt so sorry for girls like Janice and it seemed a fair thing to do.

For weeks I lay all day on my stomach and all night in a plaster cast bed. It was so hard to be strapped in tightly and made to sleep on your back! I often tried to curl up on my side, but the nurses gently woke me and put me straight! I had to sleep in that cast until I was eighteen. It should have been changed, but I stopped growing, and it fitted me all those six years!

I learned a new skill during those months. One afternoon each week a teacher came and taught us to embroider. I already liked sewing and quickly learned skills like Shadow Stitching. All through my life I have turned to embroidery for relaxation, so I am very grateful to that lady. I was also in the hospital Girl Guide troop. We were known as 'blue guides', as we were rather limited in the things we were able to do. One badge which we worked for was 'Bird Watching'. The ward had a veranda, and on sunny days the young nurses pushed our beds outside after school lessons were finished for the day. There we watched for birds in the hedges and small areas of garden around the hospital. It was also fun just to be outside and enjoy seeing something other than the grim four walls of the ward. One or two nights, when it was very warm, we were allowed to stay outside to sleep.

My experiences in that hospital taught me a lot although I didn't appreciate it at the time. When I was finally discharged I felt like a stranger in my home although I was glad to be back there. I had been so conditioned to the strict hospital routine; I suppose I had become institutionalised!

Return to School Life

Within a very few days of leaving the hospital I was back in school for the new school year. In spite of trying to keep up with the work, I had fallen behind most of my classmates. I struggled with Maths in particular, wanting to maintain my place in the first division, but it was impossible. My old fears and feelings of inadequacy flooded in again, especially when I was demoted to the lower division. I never did catch up and needed special coaching in order to obtain my 'O' level certificate a few years later.

I was developing a love for the natural sciences, especially Botany and Biology. By my mid teens I had an enormous collection of pressed wild flowers. (In those days we were allowed to pick them!) I also knew the names of many species of trees and could recognise them by their leaves. My walk to school took me through a large park - the Victoria Park, in Bath. Whatever season of the year I always enjoyed that walk and found things to interest me.

Biology became my favourite subject, and I determined to study it for 'A' level. Much to my surprise I gained seven good 'O' level passes and prepared to enter the sixth form.

I began to study Biology and delighted in the art of dissection! My little set of instruments was my prize possession. Even my brothers thought it strange that I should delight in the inside workings of a worm or a dogfish!

I had been sent a couple of times a week to help the teachers in the 'transition' part of the school where the girls of about seven to eight years were taught. The lessons were usually English and Games. I felt lost and intimidated by these noisy little girls. At the end of the first term the headmistress asked to see my parents. That was quite unusual as it was before Parents' Evenings had been invented, and certainly there was no career guidance offered. Most girls from the school were encouraged to go to college or (if they were very clever) to university and then to teach. Somehow it was an undisputed fact that I was expected to become a teacher, and now the head told my parents that I was too quiet and quite unsuitable. She suggested I left school and found some sort of job. I was not even consulted! When Mum and Dad returned from the interview and told me that I would be leaving school at the end of that term, I was devastated! I had so wanted to continue to study Botany and Biology!

So my school life ended abruptly. I didn't have many friends, but those I had I missed very much. My father talked with me about getting a job and looked into the possibility of doing Marine Biology in the Ministry of Defence. However, while he was investigating this, a post was advertised in our local paper for Junior Technician in a medical laboratory at the general hospital. I decided to apply and went through all the interview procedures. I got the job! So I began to train in Microbiology, and life began to revolve around pathogens and microscopes!

There were about six of us in the lab. This was run by the Medical Research Council. Although I was the junior of all the juniors, I liked the work and was quick to learn.

At this time, something amazing happened to me! It was the most life-changing experience a person could have. I had made friends with one of the two secretaries who did the laboratory reports. This girl, Yvonne, was a couple of years older than me and had a very friendly and bubbly personality. She had just become engaged to her young man, Jim. They both lived in a village a few miles out of town and were very involved in the youth group of the chapel there. One Saturday evening, Yvonne had invited me to go to a special event which was being held. I agreed, partly because I wanted to meet the famous Jim! I cycled over to the village and found the chapel quite easily. Yvonne and Jim met me and welcomed me, introducing me to some of their friends. Then the meeting got under way. Over the platform hung a huge banner with the words "Jesus is the answer to my every need."

My parents were Christian believers, and I had been to church since babyhood. I had never disbelieved, but the Christian message had never really touched my heart. I knew that I had a need. I longed to know Jesus in the personal way that Yvonne did. Throughout that meeting I became more and more uncomfortable. A real battle was going on in my mind. Who was going to run my life - me or Jesus? I wanted to know Jesus as a friend, but I also wanted to be boss of my own destiny. The closing moments were agony. The visiting speaker was making an appeal for people to commit their lives to Christ and come to front of the chapel as a witness to their decision. I could hardly hear his words for my heart was thumping so loudly in my chest! The final hymn was well under way before I finally made my decision and invited Jesus into my life. I didn't have the courage to go forward, but I knew that from then on my life belonged to the Lord Jesus. Somehow I also knew in my spirit that one day I would be baptised as a believer and become a missionary.

The following evening I took the bus out to Saltford village and attended the service. That evening I did have the courage when the pastor shook my hand to tell him of my decision to follow Christ. He and his young wife would encourage and disciple me in the months and years to follow. They remain dear friends to this very day. However, when I told my parents of my decision to follow Jesus, I was quite unprepared for their reaction which was negative and discouraging. For the first time in my life I had made a decision which conflicted with their wishes, and it caused many years of heartache. In some ways it made me all the stronger and helped me stand up for my convictions.

As I settled down into working in the lab I gained experience and was given my own areas of responsibility. One of these was to test the local water samples which came in each evening from the bore holes, wells and mains supplies, not only in Bath but also the surrounding villages. I had plenty of teasing about being the tester of the bath water! I also tested local milk, ice cream and pork products. These included a cut of ham from the cheek of the pig, called a 'Bath chap'. These arrived on a Thursday, and I duly took samples for testing. Then the chap was stored in a special refrigerator reserved for food samples, away from those of the patients. If my tests proved clear then on Saturday afternoon, which was my half day, I went home with a tasty ham for the family! My mother always enjoyed those Bath chaps!

Other duties were not so pleasant. One afternoon there was no senior technician available to attend a post mortem. Dr. Mann, our director, decided that I would have to go. He warned me that it would not be very pleasant, and how right he was! Armed with a box of swabs, I walked over to the morgue. It was cold and quite frightening. The pathologist was ready to begin his work, but as I looked at the deceased person on the marble slab, I almost passed out! Having got over the first shock and seen my first corpse, I found I became interested as the pathologist methodically examined the body. Every now and then he asked me for a swab, and I then labelled it, returning it to the box ready to be tested when I got back to the lab. The time passed very quickly and it was all over in a couple of hours. The body was treated with great respect and sewn up so neatly afterwards. It was a revelation to me! I took the swabs back to the lab, where Dr. Mann was waiting for me. We made smears and plated the swabs on agar to see if we could grow any bugs that might have caused the death. My boss explained to me a lot about the causes of disease and the different bacteria that were pathogenic. He was an excellent teacher, and in later years I had reason to be grateful to him for his patience and teaching.

After that incidence I was given another responsibility. I was put in charge of all the testing of samples for tuberculosis, both human and bovine. I enjoyed having my own little department to manage. I had a separate bench area to make the smears and plate up the specimens. The TB bacterium took a long time to grow so the plates were incubated for six weeks. Each Friday a van brought samples from Standish Hospital in Gloucestershire, a big centre for the treatment of TB. That usually meant I was late home on Friday evenings, but again I did not really mind because I enjoyed my work. I was never left alone; our director was always the last to leave and made sure the lab was closed up securely at the end of the day.

Twice a week the three juniors travelled by train after work to college in Bristol to study for our qualifications. After the first year I was aware that I was struggling to understand much of what was being taught because of my lack of 'A' level Chemistry. My scientific background was just too shallow. In my work I was learning Microbiology (or Bacteriology, as it was then called) but in order to qualify I needed to study Biochemistry and Haematology as well.

It was quite a dilemma for me. I began to pray about my future and ask my new friend, Jesus, what I should do. The weeks went by - loving my working days and dreading my study evenings. Then one night I had a dream. It was so clear and vivid that I can still recall it! I dreamt that I was a nurse! I could see myself dressed in a starched apron and frilly cap! I woke up, and the dream was so impressed on my mind that when I went down to breakfast I announced to my totally bemused parents that I was going to train to be a nurse!

Moving to London

After a moment's silence while she digested this information, my mother began a long tirade ending with: "Why do you want to train as a nurse? You have a very good job, near to home, with good career prospects!" "Anyway, no hospital will accept you with your health record!" she added as her trump card.

My father was quiet for a little while, and then added, "You really wouldn't make it as a nurse, Mary. Why, you even fainted when we were watching 'Your Life in their Hands' on T.V. You just don't have the stamina for that sort of job. Just forget this silly idea."

That week we had a guest staying with us: an old friend of the family, the Reverend John Page. In fact, he had been the minister who had baptised me as a five-year-old girl. He was conducting some meetings in the city for a week.

When my parents had digested my statement and given their opinions, he quietly looked at me and said, "You will be surprised by this, Mary, but I have prayed for many years that you would become a nurse!"

That silenced us all! Me, because I was dumbfounded that John Page would even think of me, let alone pray for me, and it just confirmed to me that it was the Lord who had given me that dream and done so at the very time when he was staying with us. My parents were also silenced because they respected this minister so much and trusted his spiritual judgement in many matters. Shyly, I then explained why I had made my pronouncement, telling them of my dream, before I made haste to get to work on time.

While at work I had an opportunity to tell my boss that I wanted to change course and train as a nurse. Dr. Mann then asked me to go with him to his office and talk over my decision. I was expecting more opposition but in fact found him very helpful and supportive. He understood all about my problems with the night school classes, and although he felt they could be overcome with help and were really no reason to leave the laboratory work, he also felt that my personality was very suited to a nursing career.

"To which hospital are you thinking of applying?" he asked me. I hadn't really given it much thought. I felt it would be better if I was away from home so suggested Bristol Royal Infirmary since it was not too away and was known to be a good teaching hospital.

"That sounds good, but you could also try a London hospital like Bart's or University College," he added. "Let me know how you get on, and also I will be very glad to give you a reference."

I thanked him very much, slightly bemused that so much had happened so quickly.

That lunch time I went over to the Hearing Aid Department of the hospital. I often ate my lunch with two Christian friends from Saltford

Chapel who worked there. By this time, Yvonne had left work following her marriage to Jim, and these girls had become spiritual encouragers to me. I told them of my dream and they prayed with me concerning the application to a nursing school.

I think my mother hoped that everything would soon revert to normal and that I would forget all about being a nurse! When my application to Bristol was turned down because of my medical records she was elated, and I was left very deflated and confused.

"I told you that your back condition would stop you being a nurse," she said. "You tried and the door has been shut so forget all about it and enjoy what you are doing," she advised.

I couldn't do that! I was sure that God had called me to train as a nurse so somehow I believed it would come about!

When Dr. Mann heard that Bristol had turned down my application he decided that he would look into the matter. He contacted Mr. Burton, the orthopaedic surgeon who had treated me as a child, and they went into the archives and found the notes and x-rays; then they discussed my case together. Having decided that there was nothing in my medical history that was serious enough to stop me nursing, I was once again called into the boss's office.

"Forget Bristol and apply to London," was his advice. "I will write a covering letter about your previous medical history as well as a reference. Try Bart's and University College." He went on to add, "I trained at 'Bart's, and I know the matron at UCH; she is a very kind and fair lady."

I followed his advice, and both hospitals invited me for an interview. At the end of the interview at St. Bartholomew's I was told that although I qualified in every way, I was half an inch too short for their regulations! All their nurses had to be at least five feet and two inches tall because their beds were high. There was nothing I could do about that, but I travelled home from London rather upset and fearing my mother's "I told you so!"

A week or so later I went to UCH and indeed, as my boss had promised me, the matron, Miss Downton, was a charming lady. At the end of the interview she offered me a place. She did warn me that should back trouble recur then I would have to leave and also, since many girls applied to train while they were still at school, I might have to wait a year or two to get a place. Was I willing for that?

"I don't mind how long I have to wait; I just want the opportunity to train as a nurse!" I answered. I was so delighted to be accepted!

"Then go back to work and learn all you can about microbiology," she replied. "It will be very useful to you in your career. I look forward to you becoming one of my nurses!"

Once I had the acceptance in writing, my parents also began to accept my change of career. I was sent a list of things which I would need when I began at the training school, and my mother helped me collect them. I started to knit myself the regulation grey cardigan. It encouraged me to make it even though I might have a long wait before it was worn! Finding black stockings was a different matter! They were not in fashion then, and we could not seem to find any for sale in Bath. However, an aunt, hearing of the problem, managed to acquire a couple of pairs for me. It was like getting a trousseau together!

Three months after my acceptance I received a letter from Matron's office. Could I start in three weeks' time? A new set were starting on December 31st, and one girl had dropped out at the last minute. Would I like her place? Would I indeed! Then I realised that I couldn't give a month's notice to the lab. My head was spinning! If God had opened up a place for me, then surely I would be freed to go! I went to pray with my two friends that lunchtime and then afterwards asked my boss if I could talk with him.

"What is it Mary?" he questioned. "You have been looking a bit worried all morning!"

"I have received a letter from UCH giving me a place in the next nursing school, but it starts in three weeks' time," I explained. "That means I can't give a month's notice here."

Dr. Mann's eyes crinkled and he began to smile.

"I am sure we can work something out," he said. "You must be owed some holiday anyway! If you work a bit of overtime at Christmas, because someone has to be on duty with me, then I am sure we can sort it for you!"

I felt so relieved!

Then followed three hectic weeks, which included Christmas with the family, extra working shifts and a farewell party given to me by my working mates! At last I was packed and ready to start my new life on December 31st 1959.

2

Training Days

Preliminary Training School

*A*fter Christmas, December 1959, my father and I went to the sales and bought a trunk. Then I had the fun of packing it. I had been issued with a list of essentials to bring with me to start my nursing career which I duly packed along with my 'mufti' clothes, a few treasured family photos and mementos, and a few precious books (including my Bible). There was so much which I would have like to have taken with me, but I could not pack it all into one small trunk!

New Year's Eve arrived, and my great adventure began. Dad had decided to come to London with me as I needed help with the trunk. I was so glad of his support and company! As we sat on the train taking us from Bath to Paddington, he looked kindly at me.

"Mary," he said, "if you don't like nursing, it doesn't matter. You can come home at any time".

"It's all right, Dad," I replied. "Thank you, but I will be fine!"

I didn't feel at all 'fine' inside, but I knew God had a purpose for my life that included nurse training so I felt confident I was doing the right thing. Even so, I was grateful to hear Dad's words for they made me feel loved even if I failed. However, I was determined not to fail but make my family proud of me.

The taxi from Paddington Station drew up outside the Rockefeller Nurses' Home in Huntley Street, London W1, and somewhat nervously I climbed up the steps to the imposing door. Dad followed behind me, carrying the trunk. We were greeted by a little lady in uniform who seemed even smaller than me! Her kindly smile allayed some of my fears as she led us into a sitting room. She explained she was one of the two 'home sisters' whose job it was to take care of the nurses who lived in the home. Other girls were sitting in the room along with their parents who were saying their fond farewells. As soon as I was settled my father said goodbye and left for his train back to Bath. I struggled not to cry as he kissed me, and I waved him goodbye. Neither of us has ever been very good at goodbyes. Now I was really on my own and my new life was about to begin.

When the entire new intake had arrived (and there were twenty-five of us), we were led downstairs to a small dining room. For the first three months of our training we would eat in this room as it was protected from the mêlée of the whole student nurse body. Shyly I sat at a table.

Inside I was quaking a little. The minister of my church had impressed upon me how important it was to make a stand as a Christian right from the start. I needed to 'nail my colours to the mast'.

So I knew that I should 'say grace' before I ate my meal. I bent my head and closed my eyes for a moment or two, praying more for courage than for giving thanks for the food! As I looked up, my eyes met those of another girl who sat opposite me. She was doing the same! We smiled at each other, recognising that we were both Christians, and from that moment we became firm friends.

After tea we were guided to a classroom and given a few instructions about our new lives. We were asked to share rooms. My new friend Joy and I instantly agreed to share together. It was so amazing to find a Christian friend on my very first day. God had really answered my prayers!

The next day we were measured for our uniforms. The length of our skirt hems had to be exactly twelve inches from the floor (no mini-skirts allowed!) Our hair had to be off our collar (mine was short so that was not a problem). Anyone with long hair had to have it put up (no swishing pony tails!) No jewellery was allowed except our fob watches which were pinned to our aprons, so that we could take pulses. Then we were taught how to make our pleated caps. They seemed quite complicated at first, but after practice we soon got the hang of making them. We were also issued with short, red capes to wear when outside the hospital. While we were in the Preliminary Training School (PTS) and on our first ward we were recognised by these red capes. If we survived our first six months we would be promoted to wearing long, grey capes!

Once kitted out, our training began in earnest. Classes were held all day, Monday to Friday, in the School of Nursing, and we were taught for the most part by sister tutors. In the academic classes we learnt basic hygiene and health matters, anatomy and physiology, while in the practical classroom we mastered such arts as bed making, high dusting and locker cleaning, and polishing bedpans! It was a relief to us all when we began to move on to injecting oranges with water, taking temperatures, pulses and blood pressures, and laying up dressing trays and trolleys. That seemed more like nursing! We had a dummy patient, dubbed 'Mrs. Sandbags', who was duly lifted, turned and bed-bathed several times a day, until we were all skilled and confident at these tasks. On Friday afternoons we duly walked a few blocks and attended an adult education institute where we were taught Invalid Cookery. I don't recall ever having to use the recipes we learnt (such as calves' foot jelly) but it was a relaxing afternoon at the end of the week.

The weekends were free! We made the most of those because we knew that once we were working on the wards a day off on a Saturday or Sunday would be a very rare treat! Many of our set (intakes were numbered in sets and we were 145) lived in London and the Home Counties and were able to go home; but for me, Bath was too far away and the fare too expensive. Even telephoning home was so costly that it was a rare occurrence. Several times Joy invited me to her home in Orpington, and her family were always so welcoming to me all through the years I was at UCH.

On the Sundays when I remained in London I took the opportunity to visit different churches in the locality, hearing many well known preachers and teachers of the day.

We had only been in the PTS for a few days when a piece of paper was pushed under the door of our room inviting Joy and I to come along to the Inter Hospital Nurses' Christian Fellowship (IHNCF). They held their meetings in one of the nurses' home lounges on a Thursday evening. Joy and I were very glad to go and meet other Christian nurses - some students like us, but some staff nurses and sisters. The hierarchy was meaningless as we fellowshipped together. We truly felt 'all one in Christ Jesus'. This group became a focal point in our lives all the years at UCH because often it was impossible to get to church services on a regular basis. I look back and thank God so much for that group, which became my spiritual family for four years.

After a few weeks, when we had injected enough oranges and practised enough on Mrs. Sandbags, we were allocated our first wards. We were taken by the sister tutor and introduced to the ward sister, then left in her charge for a few hours. I was sent to ward OHA. It was a gynaecological ward. Most wards were allocated two PTS nurses, but I was the only one on OHA as it was very small. The first visit was scary because now we had real patients with real needs and emotions! I was quickly introduced to the domain of the junior nurse – the sluice! I became very familiar with bedpans and basic care. It was so good to be actually helping real people at last. Somehow I began to feel like a nurse, especially when patients began to call me Nurse Morris. In those days, no first names were ever used when we were on duty!

As the weeks passed we became more and more at home on our wards and looked forward to the end of the three months in PTS after which we would be full time on the ward.

I was so fortunate. A few ward sisters were known to be 'dragons' but mine was far from that. She really cared about her patients' welfare but also about her staff. Even as the most junior of juniors, she took time to teach and encourage me. It was a wonderful start to my career.

However, instead of the usual twelve weeks on a PTS ward, I had to move after six. The ward was closed for cleaning! I was really upset! I had begun to know exactly what was expected of me and where everything was kept and was so enjoying myself. I was moved upstairs to a much larger ward: OHB. It was still a gynaecological ward so many things remained the same, but it was very unsettling. The sister on this ward, however, was not an entire stranger as she was one of the leaders of the IHNCF group. She also, like the previous sister, had very high standards of care but was also kind and fair to her staff. I soon adjusted to the new circumstances and enjoyed my work.

One particular lunchtime remains forever a memory. The ward was well staffed and not very busy. Sisters always served the lunches from a heated trolley, and we took them on trays to the patients. I was given a tray for a certain lady and Sister told me to stay with her and talk to her as she ate.

"You see, she needs the understanding and love of a Christian; stay and see if you can help her."

I cannot remember what I said to the patient or if I was really any help at all, but I was touched to be asked to talk to her. In those days spiritual needs of the patients were not often recognised as much as now.

At the completion of our three months on each ward, the ward sister had to give a report on our progress. Our first PTS wards were particularly important because if you were not up to standard you might be asked to leave. I couldn't think of anything worse than that! Already I loved my training and knew that I wanted to continue as a nurse. There were some girls who realised after three months' ward work that nursing wasn't right for them, and our set lost one or two nurses at this point. We had all become friends, and so it was sad for all of us.

Night Duty

By this time six months had already passed, and we were all given two weeks' holiday. All through our training we had no choice about when our holidays occurred. We had two weeks at the end of each six months. It was quite a lot of holiday compared with other workers at that time, but we did get very tired working long hours and trying to study as well. At least we could plan ahead! I went home to see the family. It was the first time since I had gone to London. It was lovely to see everyone again. I went up to the laboratory and visited my friends there, and it was fantastic to get back to Saltford to meet up with the chapel friends who were faithfully praying for me. I managed a couple of cycle rides with my brother Tim in the surrounding countryside. It was lovely to be back in

Somerset! I never quite got used to the noise and dirt of London. No doubt everyone was fed up with hearing me talk all about my training by the end of my holiday and was glad to see me go back!

Arriving back at the hospital we were sent to Matron's office to find out to which ward we should report. We now had to do a stretch of three months on night duty. I looked at the list and found I had been sent to the male urinary-genital ward. I was to report to Sister and work a few days there before starting night duty so that I would be familiar with the ward. My heart sank! As a child I had been a victim of some sexual abuse and just didn't know if I would cope on this ward. I had somehow hoped that I would never be sent there; UCH was such a large hospital with so many wards that I could easily have done my training without ever setting foot on it! However, I had been sent to Ward 31! I duly reported for duty. I hung my new grey cloak up in the linen cupboard and met the staff. As each new shift began, so all the nurses met in Sister's office and were briefed about the patients' conditions and our duties.

It seemed a 'bottle round' was my first task so I made my way to the sluice feeling physically sick and shaking inside. No-one else was in the sluice. I prepared the trolley, and as I went to open the door I felt a hand on my left shoulder. I turned round to see who was touching me, but there was no one. With a flash of insight I realised it was the Lord, and he was strengthening me. I would be alright! There was nothing which he and I could not cope with together. I have never forgotten that wonderful experience. If I close my eyes I can almost feel that touch now. It made all the difference, and I sallied forth with confidence!

There was a third year student nurse, a 'senior', on the ward who had a 'chip on her shoulder' about being a Northerner for some reason. She liked to make life unpleasant for junior nurses, slating them with her sharp tongue and criticising far more than she encouraged. I learnt she was also transferring to night duty, and I would be working alongside her for the whole twelve weeks! That thought didn't cheer me either! Night duty was a challenge enough as it was! My body never became used to sleeping in the day or eating in the night! I found it very hard to keep alert, especially in the early hours of the morning, and also hard to do the required study during the day.

At night the senior nurse and I looked after the ward with a second year student (called a 'middle' nurse) running between two wards and giving a hand in both. A night sister patrolled several wards, making sure everything was as it should be and helping when needed, especially checking drugs. For a week or two, the senior nurse made my life as miserable as she could. I had a job to do anything that pleased her. I tried not to answer back or become too discouraged but just quietly got on with my work. Gradually our relationship improved, and I found she was really knowledgeable. She taught me a lot, including how to make good porridge and scrambled eggs for the men's breakfast! I had to make porridge in a double boiler that slowly cooked all night. It was quite an art to get it so that it was thick and creamy, never burnt and always free from lumps!

Many of the men were recovering from surgery and usually very good-natured. I began to enjoy their banter, something I would never have thought possible before the Lord put his hand on my shoulder.

There was one night that I don't suppose my senior nurse or I will ever forget! A patient who, strictly speaking, should have been on a male medical ward had been admitted; even in those days there was a shortage of beds so patients were placed wherever they could be accommodated. This poor man was suffering from a lack of calcium. It affected his brain as well as his blood chemistry. In the middle of the night he raided the ward kitchen, stark naked, and ate all the cornflakes we had ready for breakfast, using most of the milk too. No doubt his poor body was craving the calcium from the milk, but I was wondering how I would feed all the men at breakfast! Having devoured all he could lay his hands on, this poor man then decided to try to escape, still naked, down the fire ladder and head off into Tottenham Court Road! I was left to mind the ward and contact the night sister, the middle runner and the duty doctor, while my poor senior chased after him, carrying a blanket for his modesty! Eventually a policeman helped capture the guy (who must have been freezing by then, since it was in the autumn) and returned him to the safety of the ward (and a sedatory injection from the houseman!). The next night we were relieved to find that he had been transferred to a psychiatric unit! Sharing that adventure certainly helped the relationship with my senior nurse onto a better footing, and we couldn't help laughing about it from time to time.

I found that maintaining my spiritual life through night duty was really challenging. I always felt so tired and never got into a proper routine. We worked from 10pm until 8am for ten nights in a row and then had four nights off. Although four nights off duty was a good break, it rarely seemed to come at a weekend making it possible to attend church. I used to try each Sunday to sleep as soon as I came off duty, then get up in time to go to an evening service, before going back to work. It seemed a better option than going to a morning service, when I couldn't keep my eyes open! I also tried to read a bit of the Bible each day but found it hard to remember what I had read.

The pastor from the chapel where I had made my initial commitment to the Lord had taken a new pastorate at the People's Hall, Plumstead. He and his wife were very hospitable, and I became a frequent visitor to their home on my nights off, enjoying their family life and spiritual encouragement.

Some nurses enjoyed their night duty rotas and their bodies adapted well, but for me it was always a struggle! I did, however, enjoy the relative peace and calm on the ward through the night. There were many routine jobs to be done through the quiet hours, preparing for the busy day shifts.

It was on night duty that I had my first encounter with death. Although as a Christian I had been taught about death being a door into eternity (which for believers means to be with Jesus forever) I found it deeply disturbing to see a patient die, not knowing where they stood spiritually. As nurses we were trying to preserve life, so in a way it seemed like failure when a patient died, even though in many cases it was the inevitable outcome.

One night I was asked to 'special' a dying patient. This meant to sit at his side and take care of all the immediate medical needs. As I sat with him, I held his thin, wrinkled hand in mine, trusting that the human touch would bring some comfort. Silently I prayed for him. His life slipped away quietly, and I found tears in my eyes as I pulled the curtains around him. My senior nurse helped me lay out his body - a job we had practised in the classroom but was much harder to do in reality. Then we called the porters who took the body to the mortuary. We tried not to disturb the rest of the patients. We tried to shield them from the grim reality of death, but the empty bed, newly washed and made, told its own story to the men as they woke next day.

The First Year Ends

Night duty finished, once again the students of Set 145 made their way to Matron's office to see where their next assignment was to be. I found I had been sent to one of the satellite hospitals, St. Pancras. I felt a bit downcast because I felt secure and at home in the main nurses' home at Huntley Street and didn't much like change! However, to my delight, I found that Joy was also going to St. P's (as it was fondly called), although to a different ward.

I packed all my belongings once again into my trunk, and it was transported a couple of miles to the old hospital in Camden Town. St. Pancras had once been a workhouse, and it still had that grim exterior. I was to work on the female geriatric ward (now renamed 'Senior Medicine'). On entry to the ward I noticed there was a tank of tropical fish, which I was soon to learn was Sister's pride and joy and not to be tampered with! However, I loved tropical fish as my father had always kept them and, indeed, been a breeder of certain species. Those fish cheered me up every time I went on duty, and eventually Sister allowed me to feed them when she was off duty! That was a privilege indeed!

I needed the pleasure of the tropical fish tank before I entered the ward! It was a long ward with two rows of beds, full of very elderly, frail women. The ward smelt, more than faintly, of excrement. The smell made me want to vomit. There was something very depressing about the ward, and it was with a heavy heart that I made my way to Sister's office to report on duty.

I had never had much to do with elderly people except my own two grandmothers, who had so much life in them compared to these women in the ward.

The Lord certainly had much to teach me in the next three months. Not only did I learn to physically care for these elderly folk, but I learnt to respect them and admire many of them for their courage. Some of them struggled to walk or talk, and many were incontinent. The sister taught us to treat these women with the dignity they deserved. I wonder even now at her compassion that led her to dedicate her life to caring for them in such dismal surroundings. Somehow that hospital still had the air of a workhouse about it, and all the scrubbing and cleaning with disinfectant would not eradicate the smell. In the end, I think we just got used to it and accepted it.

Our duties mostly consisted of the basic bedside nursing: bed bathing, toileting, getting women up and dressed and into a chair, then making their beds before undressing them and putting them back to bed. Often mealtimes were a real challenge; many patients needed to be fed, and there were not many nurses to do this. It was so sad to see the food getting cold before we could give it to the patient. I tried to rotate so that at least sometimes patients received hot food. Of course, in order to eat the women needed to have their teeth *in situ!* Cleaning false teeth was one of the worst tasks, and you had to be sure that they got back to the right person!

It was back-breaking work. Being small, I found it hard to turn large patients and lift them in and out of bed. I was also aware that Matron had given me a place in the nurses' school even though I had a bad medical history. I could lose that place if I had serious back problems again! Often at the end of a shift I would lie flat and pray for my backache to be relieved!

I would also pray to be able to love the unlovely. Not all the women were sweet old ladies! Some were very bitter and hard and not at all grateful for the care they received. Many felt abandoned by their families and thought they would end their days on that ward.

There were others who were great characters: their cockney wit and humour enlivened our days along with their endless stories of survival through the wars.

I spent Christmas on that ward. We had a small amount of money to buy Christmas presents for the patients. Sister put a great deal of thought into these. I remember the huge delight of one very old lady who received a fly swat. She had been a missionary in Jerusalem in her youth, and now afflicted by senile dementia she could see flies everywhere and always wanted to squat them. Her Christmas gift gave her immense pleasure, swatting imaginary flies around her bed!

Much less was known about dementia in those days, but many of our ladies were troubled by it. One dear old soul was convinced that I was her daughter, Alice, and called out to me incessantly. She also regularly saw crabs crawling up the wall! I was always being called over to deal with them. Sadly, when Alice did come to see her, she didn't recognise her at all.

One memory above all will always remain with me. It humbled me so much and taught me what a servant's heart really was. It was towards the end of a late shift, somewhere near 10 pm, when the night staff was due to arrive. The patients were all tucked up in bed when an old lady called me.

"Nurse, nurse!" she wailed.

I rushed over as quickly as I could because I didn't want her to wake everyone else up. Only a short while before, I had given her a bedpan, then tended her skin to prevent pressure sores, so I wondered what was up.

"Wee, wee, wee," she muttered. I looked, and sure enough her bed was soaking. I looked around for a helper, but no-one was free, so I went to the linen cupboard to get sheets and to the sluice for a wash bowl etc. Each bed had cot sides in case anyone fell out, so I put down one side and began to roll the wet sheet. It is really a difficult task to perform single-handed. Then I saw one of the doctors come into the ward, and he came over to me. He took off his jacket, rolled up his sleeves and began to help me to wash the lady and change the bed. He was so gentle and kind, it almost took my breath away. I was so amazed, for doctors were perceived to be far above nurses and certainly would not help with personal care or nursing tasks. I thought afterwards, "That is what Jesus would have done!"

We completed our first year with time back in the school of nursing and a short holiday. We had survived, passed the preliminary exams set by the Royal College of Nursing and were no longer junior nurses! Our promotion to the second year status was marked by a white belt, which we very proudly wore!

Widening Horizons

Early in January 1961, we had a period of smog. It was my first experience of a London fog. Most of the departments around the main hospital block were accessible through underground tunnels. When the fog descended we began to live like moles, never emerging up into the outside world which was blanketed by dense, foul-smelling, acrid fog. For me, a country girl, it was terrifying. Soon after this smog a Clean Air Act was passed, and although other fogs occurred they were not so terrible. I was working on a medical ward, and patient after patient was admitted with chronic chest disease. Sadly, many did not survive. It was my first understanding of how much our environment can affect us and also the dangers of smoking to health. It was a sad beginning to a new year.

In our second year our horizons widened, and we were allowed to work in the operating theatres and premature baby unit as well as other specialist wards. We also were given the choice of three months studying Obstetrics or Psychiatry. I opted for the former, while Joy chose the latter.

There were several theatres throughout the hospital, and I was given experience in two of them: the obstetric / gynaecological and the ear, nose and throat. I was a bit apprehensive about helping with operations, but in fact I found I liked laying up the trolleys with instruments and, in due course, holding them for the surgeon to use. I had no idea how useful all the knowledge would be when I was living in the wilds of central Africa! Much of the theatre work was very routine, as everything was prepared and packed into large metal drums to be autoclaved. I spent many hours rolling cotton wool into little balls for the drums, or testing rubber gloves to make sure they were patent before being sterilized. These are jobs that modern nurses are spared as everything comes to the theatre in pre-packed and sterile containers. Of course, emergencies could arrive at any time, and then it was 'all hands on deck' for all the staff. Some of the surgeons were very patient with the student nurses and told them what they were doing and why. In that way we learnt far more than from our text books. Others were less than patient and prone to throw instruments around the room if they were annoyed!

I especially loved my time on the obstetric wards. Every time a baby was born I found tears of wonder in my eyes. Of course there were times of sadness too when the outcome was not what we all would have wanted. In a large teaching hospital such as UCH patients were referred to us as 'a centre of excellence'. Many of these women had complications in their pregnancy or a very poor obstetric history. It was especially rewarding when at long last these parents had their longed-for baby! As student nurses we were not able to deliver babies, but my time on those wards certainly encouraged me to think about midwifery training.

One day a very young mother was admitted to the ward from the casualty department. She was a girl from Eastern Europe, which was quite unusual in those days of the cold war.

With her limited English she told us that she was working as a chamber maid in a hotel. She had no idea that she was pregnant and thought perhaps she had appendicitis when the labour pains began! She went to casualty because of her pain and was so shocked when she was told that she was in labour and the baby was well on its way!

She delivered a normal, healthy little boy. When the mothers on the ward heard her story, they all began to give this young girl some of their baby clothes and nappies. Her gratitude was enormous! I think she had expected to be shunned; to be an unmarried mother in the 1960's still carried a huge stigma. We kept that girl on the ward for as long as we were able, to give her time to get over the shock and think about her future. Eventually she decided to keep her baby and return to her homeland - but not before she had been told the facts of life by Sister!

Night duty came round once again. I dreaded it because I slept so badly. I had a room in a smaller nurses' home that was alongside the obstetric hospital, and it was certainly quieter than the main Rockefeller Home. I was working on the premature baby unit. In the days before the development of special care baby units, our hospital had one of the best wards in England for caring for sick and pre term babies. How I loved these tiny babies! As I fed them I prayed for them, for their survival and for their families. They stayed with us until they were five pounds in weight, so we really grew to know those babies as the weeks went by. It was amazing how their individual personalities began to be revealed even at such an early age!

One tiny boy was born with an inguinal hernia, and it was decided that it should be repaired when he was about two weeks old. I stayed up that day and went to the viewing gallery of the theatre, where the medical students watched surgery, so that I could see his operation. I was amazed at the surgeon's huge hands managing to perform the surgery on such a tiny, tiny baby! The little boy recovered well, and I was still on the ward when he was discharged home to the care of his loving family.

The premature baby unit offered a three month course for trained nurses. At the time when I was working there, three staff nurses arrived. They were friends and had trained at King's College Hospital, London, together. They were all committed Christians, and I enjoyed getting to know them. Two of the girls were sisters and had grown up in China as missionary children. They inspired me with their tales of missionary life. They also helped to run a children's club near The Oval in South London and soon had me going along and helping, too. It was an eye-opener for me to get to know the children who came from very deprived homes in some of the tenement blocks of that area. We took them away for a weekend camp, sleeping on the floor of a church hall on the south coast. The children were very excited and quite difficult to control. One girl presented me with a lovely bouquet – picked from the local park flower beds! I stayed helping with those children whenever I was free for the rest of my time at UCH, long after the three King's nurses had left.

Those three staff nurses had also planned to go to the Keswick Convention together, staying in a house party run by a missionary society. I was due my annual holiday, so they asked me to join them. It was a wonderful experience for me. The meetings were so inspiring! At a missionary meeting I stood up, dedicating my life for missionary service, as the Lord directed.

We also had wonderful times exploring the Lake District together. I shall never forget that holiday!

On each ward I seemed to meet other Christians and form deep friendships, many of which have lasted all my life. The IHNCF meetings were very precious to us, but also we went to some of the Hospital Christian Union meetings, which doctors, medical students and other health professional attended. I became very friendly with one particular medical student. We had very little money to go on dates but had a lot of fun exploring London. We liked to walk in the docklands and try to guess what was in the warehouses by using our sense of smell! We attended the same church, St.Mary's Islington, and became 'Islington Visitors'. In this capacity I met the most amazing old lady. She was a double amputee and lived in an attic room of an old Victorian house. She was always cheerful and very pleased to see me in spite of the fact that her previous 'visitor' had been the famous cricketer and clergyman, Rev. David Shepherd! She was very proud that he had been her visitor and told me about him every time I went there. I used to have to climb up so many stairs to reach her room. Sometimes she needed something from the shops, and I would have to go up and down them an extra time. The lady had not been able to leave her room for years, yet remained cheerful and thankful for the little she had in life.

St. Mary's church also had a medical mission attached, run at that time by a physician, Dr. Metters. A group of us young people from the church went to the mission to help out and also for Bible studies when we were free, and we learned a great deal both medically and spiritually from this gentle man of God.

Friends, Relations and Finals!

Once we had graduated from being middle nurses and were given our striped belts, we had more responsibly as third year senior student nurses. Not only were we expected to be able to do more or less any procedure on the wards, but also we were now helping to supervise and train other nurses as well as study for our finals. We were working towards two sets of final exams: those set by the hospital and those for our state registration as nurses. The hospital exams were taken first and deemed the most difficult, so if we passed those then hopefully we would make the state ones! We had a month each year, as a set, in the school of nursing. We looked forward to these times when we would all be together again. This also meant evenings and weekends off, which was a great treat! When we were in 'block' we had formal lectures, many of them given by medical staff as well as our sister tutors. We also had tutorials on the wards.

Sometimes these were given by the sister tutors who came to visit us in our working location, and at other times they were given by the ward sister. After lunch the patients were encouraged to rest, and if the ward was not too busy it was an ideal opportunity for the sister to teach us about the patients' conditions. As we had progressed through the years of training our strengths and weaknesses had been noted by the ward sisters in their ward reports. A kind ward sister giving one-to-one help to a student nurse could make so much difference if she was struggling in any way.

My friendship with Joy was still very close, and we both had several other good friends. Nearly always on my day off I had someone to go out with, but even if I did not I had elderly relatives who lived near the hospital. My father had a widowed aunt and her bachelor brother living in a flat near St. Pancras railway station. I tried to find time most weeks to stop by and greet them. They were definitely people of their generation, and a very formal tea party was always conjured up when I arrived. In the tiny flat, Auntie Ada produced lace tablecloths and napkins, fine bone china tea cups and plates, along with little sandwiches and dainty cakes. It was all a world apart from our nurses' dining room! Uncle Joe had been in the Army Medical Corps in India during the war and loved to regale me with stories of his exploits. Auntie Ada used to reprimand him severely for talking about such things at tea time! They were a quaint old couple, but they were always so proud of me, telling all their neighbours that their great niece was at the 'University' (as they called the hospital). In her old age my aunt had begun to attend a mission church, a branch of Bloomsbury Baptist Church. She found comfort from the services, and the deaconess in charge helped her to find a personal faith before she eventually died.

During this third year my younger brother, Tim, came up to visit for a week. He stayed with Auntie Ada and Uncle Joe, and we went exploring London when I was off duty. He was fourteen, so it was quite an adventure to have a week in the city. We went one day to the Lord Mayor's Show, queuing up for a while but getting a very good view. Since I rarely got home, it was great to have Tim visit me! Sometimes, as adults, we have reminisced about this visit. Tim's lasting memory was watching the trains leaving St. Pancras station as he looked out of the flat window.

Early in my third year I was sent to a branch hospital in Devonshire Street. There were only a couple of wards: one for patients with ophthalmic conditions and the other for patients with tuberculosis. I worked on both of the wards. We lived in very small nurses' home nearby; being a small community we got to know each other very well and it was a little less hierarchical.

I wasn't known as a very outgoing person, but on Shrove Tuesday I decided it would be fun to have a pancake party. Having gained permission to hold it in the nurses' home lounge, everyone became involved and enthusiastic. Even the cook made some special fillings for the pancakes, which was a great treat! It was really fun!

I was transferred to night duty on the TB ward. Although TB was no longer the rampant killer as it had been in the early twentieth century, we still had a full ward. All the patients were infectious so they needed barrier nursing. I seem to recall one of my first evening jobs was to boil up all the crockery in a large steam sterilizer. All my knowledge of microbiology and my cultures from the TB hospital in Gloucestershire now made sense as I nursed these patients.

When I had made my initial commitment to the Lord about four years previously, I had known that I should be baptised by immersion, but up until this time my parents had refused permission. Now I was approaching my twenty-first birthday, and so I felt that I could ask my minister to baptise me. He was still pastor at Plumstead and only too delighted to include me in his next baptismal service. One of my UCH friends, Sue, acted as my helper while a few others came to witness my confession of faith. The date was fixed for a Sunday evening in April and all I needed to do was to ask for my nights off to cover that time. I went to the night sister at Devonshire Street asking her permission to have that time off duty. She was delighted to hear my reason for asking and willingly granted my request. My baptism was a very wonderful time. I felt the Lord come upon me and his Spirit fill me. There was a new depth to my Christian life from that day on. Sadly, my parents never understood and opposed my believer's baptism all their lives. It was one of the sad things that came between us.

For my last ward as a student nurse I was sent to the female trauma ward. This was mostly orthopaedic surgery following accidents. It was always busy, and we never knew who might be admitted at any time. Almost always we were squeezing extra beds into every available space! The sister on that ward was so good to all her staff, always seeing the best in everyone and trying to extend their skills and confidence. It was a good ward to be on when I was taking finals, for although it was hard work, it was very stimulating and the sister so supportive.

Once finals were taken, we were able to submit our preferences for the ward we would like to work in as staff nurse. We didn't always have our requests granted, and the ward sister also had to agree, but I was very fortunate in being allowed to stay on the female trauma unit. In our original contract with the hospital we signed for four years' training: three to gain our SRN and the fourth to be trained as a staff nurse. We only received our hospital certificate and badge if we completed the four years.

When the results of the hospital finals were posted on the notice board, much to my amazement I had achieved very good grades and was very near the top of the list! Even with this encouragement I still dreaded the results of state finals coming. What if I had failed? It didn't bear thinking about! When the day came we all lined up anxiously at the nurses' home 'post office', where we collected our mail. Most of the set were there tearing open their envelopes. I crept into the toilet and opened mine alone, but I need not have worried; I had passed! However, my joy was tinged with sadness for the two girls in the set who failed. They must have been so disappointed. At least they could sit the exams again in three months.

The Nursery

Times were changing in the sixties and the hospital's attitude to student nurses changed too. The rule had always been that students must be resident in the nurses' home until either they were qualified or had passed their twenty-first birthday, which was at that time the 'coming of age'. There were also strict rules concerning the time of night when nurses had to be in the home and the doors were locked. A late pass could be obtained but not too often!

While I was in my third year, the rule was eased, making it possible for us to live away from the hospital during our third year. A few years later they even allowed nurses to get married while in training!

Some of my friends from the IHNCF, a year ahead of me, had moved into a flat at West Hampstead. They christened the flat 'The Nursery'. They needed another flatmate to make up the number and invited me to join them. I prayed about it, and although it would squeeze the finances considerably I decided to live out. Flats were very hard to come by. However, if I joined them and time came for them to leave, I could invite Joy and some of our other friends to join me in the flat. My godfather generously lent me the money I needed for a deposit, and I packed my trunk one last time and moved in.

The flat was in a large house in West End Lane, not too far from the tube station that took us to UCH. It did mean waking earlier in order to get to work on time, and also getting home later, but it was worth it! We all got on very well together and shared the housekeeping without many arguments! I took on a cleaning job in order to help the finances, but it was a strain doing that as well as study and ward work. My employer was a Jewish lady and very exacting, but in the course of time we became friends, and she was upset when eventually I gave up cleaning for her.

I was also taking driving lessons. These were anything but a joy! I am not a natural driver and hated the London traffic. I took the test in North London and failed. I decided to forget driving for the time being.

My flatmates were nearing the end of their contracts at UCH, and they all had decided to move on to do further training or take posts elsewhere. I was sorry to lose their companionship and fellowship but was delighted when Joy, along with our friends Jeannette, Heather and Margaret came to join me. We all settled in and got on well together. I had a little kitten called Josephine (named thus because her brother was called Napoleon). She was a very well-behaved little cat and a welcome addition to our home.

We didn't really get to know our neighbours for we worked pretty unsociable hours. In the flat beneath us was an actress, and she communicated from time to time by little notes pushed under our door, reminding us that, "We in the theatre need to sleep late so don't make a noise in the morning!" We never knew the woman's name; we just called her Miss 'We in the theatre'! We did try to be quiet, but five nurses and a cat could not keep completely silent.

During our year as staff nurses we all needed to think about the next stage in our careers. The five of us in The Nursery decided that we would do our midwifery training. This was arranged in two parts, each lasting six months. Joy, Jeannette and I applied to go to Leicester Royal Infirmary for part one and Heather and Margaret to Shoreham on Sea. Jeannette and I were due to go for an interview on the same day in Leicester and for some reason (probably chronic lack of funds) decided to hitchhike there! I guess it was still safe to do that, but even now I wonder at our boldness! By God's grace we not only reached Leicester safely and in time for the interviews but also found lifts back to London and arrived home safely! We were all given places in our chosen training hospitals and looked forward to being together for the next stage of our nursing.

One day I had a message from Matron's office. Would I please go and see her! I wondered what I had done; I automatically presumed I must have done some misdeed and needed a reprimand! I racked my brain as to what it was but couldn't think of anything. By the time I arrived in Matron's office I was shaking at the knees!

"Sit down, Nurse Morris," she invited. She didn't look severe and inwardly. I sighed with relief; perhaps I wasn't in trouble!

"I know you will be surprised at this news," she continued, "for you are quiet and unassuming. The Hospital Trust has decided to award you the gold medal. Each year one nurse is chosen not only for her academic success but also on her ward reports, her attitude and even how tidy she has kept her room in the nurses' home!"

I sat there totally dumbfounded. I knew one or two nurses whose aim had been to get the coveted gold medal. It hadn't even occurred to me. Matron was right in that it came as a total surprise, and I sat there in shock!

"At the prize-giving you will give the vote of thanks to Lady Reading, our guest, who will present the certificates and prizes. I will need to read it through when you have prepared it. Please make an appointment to see me when you have it ready... and congratulations!"

"Thank you" I replied, still in shock; then asked "Can I tell my friends and family?"

"Yes, of course. Now that I have talked to you it can be public knowledge. I will also tell your ward sister."

In a daze I returned to The Nursery. When I arrived home one of my flat mates was off duty and immediately wanted to know why I had been summoned to Matron's office. I was embarrassed and really struggled to tell her about the award, although I was thrilled about it. It was easier to phone my parents and tell them. They were delighted and, of course, came to the prize giving. I hated all the fuss but it was an honour and one I knew only the Lord could have brought about. It was he who had brought me into nursing and kept me all through the years!

Midwifery Training

I had almost completed my year as a staff nurse and was looking forward to Part One Midwifery Training with Joy and Jeannette when I fell sick with glandular fever. Although I wasn't too long recovering, I didn't feel quite ready for the move to Leicester so I postponed the course for six months. Moving to Leicester was like moving to a foreign country because I knew no-one there and struggled even to understand the accent! The intake of student midwives was quite small, and we all came from different hospitals. I made friends with an Indian nurse called Pramilla. She was a Hindu, and we had many interesting discussions during our six months together. Many of our patients were from Indian or Pakistani backgrounds, and she helped me understand more about their cultures and religions.

The hospital was basically a group of old cottages knocked into one! It was called Bond Street. It was an awkward building to work in, with narrow corridors and steps in odd places. There was an annexe to the hospital, called 'The Vicarage' because it was located in a house which had previously had that function. Although the buildings were far from ideal, the staff was a close-knit community, dedicated to help mothers during childbirth. When we arrived we had an initial time in study block with the midwifery tutor before we were let loose on the wards. Then we had to observe a certain number of deliveries before we were allowed to deliver babies under supervision by ourselves. We also had to learn how to care for mothers during pregnancy and postnatally.

I enjoyed the six months and loved studying midwifery. The hospital was always very busy so I gained plenty of experience in deliveries. The required amount before our exams was ten, but I probably delivered ten times that number! I was very thankful when working in the Congo for all the experience and also the good teaching I had received at Bond Street. God was preparing me for the future!

The nurses' home was a friendly place, but I struggled spiritually. Although I visited several churches, rarely did anyone speak to me or welcome me. It taught me a lesson to try to look out for newcomers and welcome them once I was settled in a church! The hospital tried to persuade me to stay in Leicester and do the second part of my training at a nearby hospital, but I wanted to go back to the West Country! I felt it was time to be nearer my family, particularly as I was sure I would eventually be living abroad. I applied to a very small hospital in Bradford-on-Avon. It was not too far from my home and set in beautiful countryside. The nurses' home was in an old manor house, which was such a joy to live in! For this part of the training we spent three months hospital-based and three months on the district with a supervisory midwife. My time in the hospital was very enjoyable apart from one thing: the food! We had an ex-RAF chef who seemed to have a penchant for beetroot and bananas! Beetroot was served so often, both hot and cold. Bananas, especially banana custard, seemed to be a dessert served almost every other day! Maybe that too was to be missionary training for future years!

This move meant that once again I would have to make friends in a new place. Most of the pupil midwives were local girls, and there was no problem with the Wiltshire accent!

Although Bradford-on-Avon Maternity was a small hospital, it served a wide, rural area, and we were usually quite busy. I certainly had more than the required number of deliveries. I recall one night looking after a young mother in labour with her first child. We delivered a little girl and were waiting for the placenta to be delivered when she gave a big push and out came, to everyone's surprise, a second baby! She had undiagnosed twins! Fortunately, all was well and both babies very healthy. Her husband had to be treated for shock when he heard the news! A large, strong cup of tea was in order! His bank balance also suffered when he had to go shopping the following day to buy for two children instead of one!

There was a practice in that hospital which I did not encounter anywhere else in my nursing career. The babies were not bathed, only oiled after birth and each subsequent day with a cold cream lotion. They always looked and smelled lovely. Even to this day I am not sure whose idea it was, but it worked well! The mothers stayed in hospital at least a week after delivery. We helped them to bond with their babies and establish feeding. They were shown how to bath the babies just before they went home so that they knew what to do! No one seemed to mind staying so long in hospital. Apart from the beetroot and bananas they had good food and lived in a beautiful old manor house surrounded by lovely gardens!

I worked on the wards for two months by day, then a month on nights. In those days all the babies were taken at night to a large nursery so most of our night was spent in there. We gave any bottle feeds that were required and woke the mothers who were breast feeding when needed. There were always two pupils and one trained midwife on duty through the night, and the pupils took turns in doing deliveries. We learnt to use forceps and a suction pump when necessary. The local GP was on call should here be real problems, and any other emergencies were sent by ambulance to Bath.

I had my bicycle with me in Bradford-on-Avon, and in spite of the hills, I cycled into Bath for my days or nights off, re-establishing contacts with friends and spending time with my family. I had asked to do my final three months of district training in Bath, and this request was granted. I lived at home, and my parents were very good putting up with the night calls and my coming and going at odd times. When the midwife who was to be my supervisor came to the house to visit me, she and my mother discovered they knew each other! My mother had taken her and her sister to Sunday school in Weymouth when they were small girls!

Working on the district I was supposed to use my bike to get around to my patients each day. Bath is built on seven very steep hills! I seemed to end up pushing the bike more than I rode it! When I was called out at night, the midwife would always come by car to collect me, and she kindly took pity on me sometimes when I had a visit to do that was a long way from home.

Delivering babies at home was a very different scenario from doing it in hospital. The responsibility lay heavily upon me because there was no doctor close at hand and, in those days, not such a good emergency service. At first, my senior midwife accompanied me to each delivery, but eventually I had to go alone in order to prove my competence. My worst scare was when I had to deliver a baby in a basement flat in one of the old Georgian houses near the centre of Bath. The father was in the RAF, and he and his young wife were expecting their first baby. When I was called, the mother was well into her labour and ready to deliver. The father was busy doing all the right things: boiling water, etc. The baby's head delivered slowly, and it was large. The shoulders then turned, but they stuck and just would not deliver. I asked the father to phone for the doctor and senior midwife. Not everybody had phones at home, and this poor young man had to run down the road with the coins in his hand to the local phone box. I meanwhile was trying to put some gentle traction on the shoulders, scared lest the poor mother tear. I was praying silently, and mercifully the Lord answered. I managed to get the shoulders out and an eleven pound baby boy delivered safely before the doctor or midwife arrived! I was so thankful! The poor mother was exhausted! She had torn, but only a little, and the doctor praised me for a good job! It brought home to me what an awesome responsibility it was to bring a baby into the world.

Although I loved my training as a midwife, I knew it was time to make decisions about my future. What was to be the next step in my life? Right from the time when I committed my life to Christ in Saltford Chapel, I knew for me that commitment would mean baptism by immersion and missionary service. I had been baptised, but was it now time to move into missionary work? I talked to my father, who had always had a great interest in missionary work. He advised me to apply to a Bible College. I was due to finish midwifery at the end of August 1965, so perhaps I could start in college the following September. I applied to Dalton House Bible College in Bristol - a ladies' college which was linked with the Bible Churchman's Missionary Society (BCMS). I also applied to the Bath City Council for a grant. I didn't think there was much chance of getting a grant, but Dad said it was worth a try, so I did. I was surprised when, not only did I get a place in the college, but also a full grant was awarded! So it looked as if I would be at college the following September. However, God had other plans!

One day in July I was idly looking through the adverts in the Nursing Mirror when suddenly I became arrested by one. It just 'leapt out of the page' at me! I was also quite disconcerted because my future path had just been settled; yet here was an advert which I couldn't take my eyes off! I tried to forget it and focus on other things, but I could not. I should have been revising for my final midwifery exams, but the advert kept intruding on my thoughts. In the end, I thought perhaps God was speaking to me. I asked him to somehow tell me if he was leading me into a new avenue.

The advert was placed by the Medical Research Council (MRC); they were looking for a sister to work in the infantile malnutrition unit in Kampala, Uganda. They hoped to fill the post in September and applications needed to be sent in at once. The applicants also needed a clean driving licence. I was still having lessons!

I had been at Bradford-on-Avon hospital for a tutorial and was taking the bus back to Bath. The journey took about forty minutes so I had taken with me a new publication, 'Living Letters'. It was a paraphrase of the Epistles. I was reading Colossians, and once again something on the page 'leapt out at me'! It said: "Go to those in urgent need."

I was staggered! It was as if God had spoken out loud to me. I knew it was his answer. Who could be needier than malnourished infants in Uganda? Then, I thought, "What will people think? Here I am with a place in college and even a grant to go there, and now I want to go to Uganda!"

When I arrived home, Dad could tell that something was on my mind.

"What's troubling you?" he asked.

I told him. I expected him to be very disapproving but to my surprise he wasn't at all!

"In these days I think there are so many opportunities for missionary work other than the traditional missionary societies," he commented. "I think it sounds a very good idea. Why don't you apply? If you get the post you will know it was God's leading; if you don't, then college still waits."

With Dad's encouragement I applied, and even though I had no driver's licence I was successful in getting the job. I quickly put in for a driving test, wrote to the college and told them the change of plans. The principal was most helpful and suggested that I do a correspondence course with them while I was abroad, which would give me the basic college certificate. I agreed to do that but cancelled the city council grant.

3

Africa

Off to Uganda

I only had a few weeks to prepare for my new life in Africa. First, there were the injections necessary for foreign travel. Then I needed to purchase most of what I might need for the next two years. How much toothpaste would I need? What would be available locally? Then there was the dreaded driving test! Once again, to my mortification, I didn't pass! Would that jeopardise my appointment? Fortunately it didn't. I learnt that the reason for needing to be a driver was because the hospital was some distance from the staff residences, and it wasn't suitable to walk, especially after dark. I was told that I could take a test in Kampala. I later learned what that would involve!

Finally all the preparations were complete, and I was ready to take leave of my family. We all went to the very newly opened Chinese restaurant in Bath for a farewell meal. That was a new experience for my parents! My mother and father came to see me off at Heathrow Airport. In those days there was a viewing platform, and as I boarded the aeroplane I could see them waving from the distance.

Suddenly all my excitement evaporated and I thought, "What have I done?!"

I felt really scared at the thought of travelling to East Africa on my own. I had never before flown - let alone half way across the world. However, friends at home were praying for me; the panic subsided, and I felt at peace. I had received such clear guidance that I knew the Lord was with me and all would be well.

At Entebbe Airport I was met by a nurse working at the unit who had also trained at UCH. Although I didn't know her I did recognise her face, and it was so good to have a common link. I was taken to my accommodation: a flat which I was to share with Jennifer, one of the unit's secretaries. Although she had arrived in Uganda just the day previous to me, it was her second tour of duty and she knew the ropes. How glad I was of that! She and I became firm friends and remain so to this day.

It was very exciting to live and work in Africa. Uganda was a newly independent country and Britain's gift at Independence had been Mulago Hospital. Our unit, however, used one of the old hospital's (now redundant) wards. The unit consisted of a ward with eight cots, a sister's office, a laboratory where the biochemists and doctors worked, and an office where the secretaries worked. There were also a few small rooms for storage etc. We were a small staff: four nursing sisters, all from the UK; a couple of Ugandan nurses; cleaners; an interpreter; the office staff; two doctors; and a nutritionist and biochemist. Fortunately we all got on well together.

It took me a while to learn and understand the research which was being undertaken and the special responsibilities which we nurses had. I was shocked at the degree of malnutrition in our small patients - to see an eight-month-old baby who weighed only eight pounds! It was very frustrating not to be able to speak Luganda, the principle language of the area. We learnt just a few words, but they were little more than the common greetings.

After a very short while, a driving test was arranged for me, and I had to take a couple of lessons with a Ugandan teacher. It was 'a hair-raising experience'! Driving in Kampala was definitely not like driving in Somerset! A required feature of the test was to reverse park between two bollards at the test centre. If you failed at this point the rest of the test was abandoned. The same applied if you failed on the knowledge of the Ugandan Highway Code, also tested before you left the centre.

I had been informed by many Europeans and Africans alike that I would need a large bribe in order to pass. White people were failed on principle, so that more fees could be charged for another test, unless a fat bribe went to the tester! What was I to do? Bribing was immoral and out of the question. I wrote home to my Christian friends about the dilemma and asked them to pray on the day of the test. They did. Praise God, I passed with no bribes given! When I returned to the unit there was genuine amazement because I had told them that I would not pay a bribe so they had expected me to fail.

Now there was the fun of buying a car! I knew nothing about cars so was extremely grateful for the help of one of the male members of the unit who looked for a good car for me. I ended up with a grey Volkswagen Beetle which I named 'Lucy'. She was a faithful friend for the two years spent at the unit.

I needed to find a spiritual home. I found that there were services in English at All Saint's Cathedral in the centre of the city and began to worship there. I found that many other ex-patriots worshiped there and began to make some friends - including a teacher called Alison. Alison helped with a Girl Crusader Bible Class and asked me if I would help her as well. I was glad to do so since as a girl I had enjoyed being a Crusader myself. Some Sundays I was working but not every week.

At Christmas I had some leave and made a safari in 'Lucy' to Karamoja, a region in the north east of the country. It was a long trip and quite a challenging adventure for me. I knew one of the BCMS missionaries, a teacher in that region, and she had invited me to stay at the mission station at Amudat. There was a hospital there, and she was going to join other missionary friends for the festival. The region was so different from Kampala - very hot and dry, sparsely populated by nomadic tribal herdsmen. I was fascinated by the Karamajong and Pokot tribes' people and their culture. It was wonderful to see the missionaries helping them and sharing with them the love of God.

After Christmas I left my friend, Sylvia, and headed over the border to Kenya to visit another missionary who had at one time been my Girl Guide captain in Bath. She worked in the church also among the Pokot people. I stayed a night with her at a place called Kapenguria, then continued to visit one more friend further south, at Eldoret, before crossing the border and driving back to Kampala. It had been quite an adventure! Looking back I realise how good God was to me, for I had no punctures or mechanical trouble apart from some wet plugs after I had forded a river. Petrol had been available in every station *en route* and I arrived back safe and sound!

Not long after this great adventure I met an old acquaintance from my London training days. I had been to church at All Saints, one Sunday morning, and after the service realised that I recognised one of the young men coming out of the porch. It was Keith Waddell, whom I had met when he and my then boyfriend shared a flat. I had no idea that he had come to Africa and was now a missionary doctor with Africa Inland Mission (AIM) in the south west of Uganda. Little did I know it then, but he was to play a significant role in my life!

Keith was very interested in the research which the unit was doing and made several visits to us. He also invited me to go to see the missionary hospital where he was working. I arranged to do this on a weekend off, but rather than drive down to the south west I decided to go by train, mostly for the fun of the experience. A passenger train ran between Kampala and Kasese; sadly it no longer runs. The train took all day, and I travelled third class, so was squashed in amongst lots of people, chickens and all sorts of baggage! At most of the stations *en route* the carriage would empty, the passengers disembarking to buy provisions like roast corn, roast rats on sticks, peanuts and drinks. Eventually we arrived at Kasese, and I was glad to see Keith waiting for me. We drove through the copper mines close to the border with Rwanda where he was working in two small hospitals, Nyabirongo and Kagando. Eventually, the work expanded and Kagando became the main hospital base. The missionaries lived in the small village of Nyabirongo: just a cluster of little houses and a few clinic buildings. There were two older, single American nurses and an American doctor and his wife stationed there. The weekend I visited, the doctor and his wife were on leave, so I didn't meet them.

It was late by the time we arrived as we had stopped for a meal in the lovely Hotel Marguerita which overlooked the beautiful Ruwenezori Mountains. I was very tired and it was dark, so with the aid of a kerosene lamp I settled into a little hut and fell soundly asleep. After an hour or so I was woken by a strange noise, and it seemed to me in my dreamy state that I was in a London Underground train. Then the rumbling became intense, and Keith and the two nurses were knocking at my door urging me to get out of the house as we were being shaken by an earthquake! Fortunately nobody was hurt and there was no structural damage to the mission station, but it was quite a frightening experience. A nearby town did suffer considerable damage, and the quake was felt as far away as Kampala, where it set off the burglar alarms in many cars, causing chaos and panic!

Eventually we all went back to bed, only to be woken again in the early hours by insurgent soldiers from Rwanda who lived in the mountains. There had been some fighting and the soldiers had brought in some of their wounded colleagues. Keith asked if I would help him in the operating theatre. Of course I agreed, and we spent some hours extracting bullets and sewing up wounds.

Fortunately the Sunday proved a quieter day, and we went to the church at Kagando. Then I was able to see the hospital there before Keith drove me to Kampala in his small car. On the way we became stuck in a muddy pothole. It took a lot of men and boys to help push us out so that we could continue on our way.

It was quite an eye-opener into the life of a missionary! Did I really want that level of excitement in my life?

Changes

Jennifer and I enjoyed sharing an apartment together. However, she had other important things happening in her life. On her previous tour of duty she had met a young engineer: Graham. They both enjoyed sailing on Lake Victoria. The friendship had progressed through the months. After her return he proposed marriage, and she happily agreed. This meant that she would cut short her contract and return to UK. Before she went we had a weekend together in Nairobi. We drove there, via Lake Naivasha, in order to see the flamingos and then explored the wonderful capital city of Kenya. We also had a night at Thompson Falls, which was spectacular. It was so good to have that time together before she went home to be married.

Our next-door neighbour at that time was a certain Ugandan army colonel called Amin. Not that we had any invitations to dine at his house; rather we were a bit intimidated by the soldiers who guarded his compound. Little did we know what havoc that man would wreak upon the country!

All this time I tried to keep studying, doing the Bible diploma papers for Dalton House College as I had promised and also going to typing classes a couple of times a week. I enjoyed the Bible study but was not so good with the typewriter! However, those classes proved their worth when the age of computers was born. At least I knew my way around a keyboard even though I didn't ever manage to touch type.

There was a change in my own life too. Keith had been visiting Kampala and, as he always did, met up with me for a meal and a chat. He was staying at the CMS missionary guest house at Namirembe Cathedral with another AIM missionary from the north of Uganda. This young man came from my home town of Bath. Keith and I had arranged to swim at the pool on the university campus so he asked if he could bring Phil Weeks with him. So began a friendship with Phil which was to change my life.

Our friendship blossomed as Phil began to order the manual and leaflets which I needed to teach the Crusader class through the bookstore which he ran in Arua, West Nile. Soon he began to visit Kampala regularly, and I also went up to visit him at the mission station where he worked.

About this time Jennifer returned to England to get married to Graham. Rather than stay in the apartment on my own, it was decided that I would move up to the apartments where the other nurses lived. The move was just a few doors up the road. I was to share a flat with another nurse, Sylvia, a Welsh girl who had come out to the unit just a few months after me. Sylvia was a very pleasant and also very talented girl, and we got on well together. There was just one area of difficulty and that was that she was very anti-God and anti-the-church. A few years previously her fiancé had been at theological college but had been tragically killed in a road accident. This had left her broken and bitter and she had discarded the faith she had once had.

Phil was from a Baptist background and on one of his visits introduced me to the Kampala Baptist Church. The American Missionary couple who were ministering there at the time, Rev. Lynn and Mrs. Marcelyn Holm, became my very special friends. Marcie was like a big sister to me and in many ways became my spiritual mother. I owe so much to her for she continued to be my spiritual mum right up until her death in 2006.

When we first met, the Holms' had five young children who quickly became my adopted nephews and nieces. I was made to feel part of the family, and we had lots of fun together.

They also opened their home to Phil so that when he came to Kampala he didn't have to stay in the guest house.

As our friendship deepened into love, Phil asked me if I would be his wife. His proposal was somewhat unusual. He wrote and told me to go and buy the number 1 hit record in the Uganda charts. I was very puzzled at this but went to the record shop. The little EP record was Jim Reeves singing 'Distant Drums', and as I listened, the first line of the chorus was "Oh, Mary, marry me!" When I gave him a positive answer he explained that he would like to ask God for a sign that our engagement was in his plan. Phil had experienced the trauma of a broken engagement some years previously and didn't want to make a second mistake; after all, we were in a rather unnatural situation living so far from home. I agreed, and we decided to ask the Lord to soften Sylvia's heart and bring her back to faith. When that happened we would buy a ring. Looking back, maybe it was not a very mature request to make; I don't know. It was certainly bold! The Lord was so good to us and so gracious.

Timidly, the following Sunday I asked Sylvia if she would like to come with me to the Baptist Church. She had come from a Welsh chapel background so I felt she would be at home in that kind of service. My faith was weak, for I was very surprised when she accepted the invitation. We went to the evening service, and she was deeply moved, asking to talk to Lynn, the pastor, at the end. We went to Holms' home, and that evening Sylvia gave her life to the Lord.

I couldn't wait to tell Phil! I wrote a letter to him at once, and his reply was to appear the next weekend and whisk me to the jewellers to buy a ring! We telephoned home to my parents for Phil to ask for my hand. My parents knew about our friendship, but it was the first time Phil had spoken to my father. There was so much rejoicing. Very soon after this the telephone lines were extended into West Nile where Phil was working, and we were able to communicate more easily. That proved a blessing in many ways but none more so than when I caught a virus and became sick very quickly. I appeared to have viral encephalitis. I was taken into a medical ward in Mulago Hospital, and Phil was sent for. I guess I must have been pretty sick for this to happen, but I don't remember very much! My physician was Dr. John Billinghurst, and I am very grateful to him. Many years later we met up again as he was a dear friend of my second husband.

So many exciting things happened during those years in Uganda, from seeing elephants and crocodiles in the wild to writing my first published case histories in the Nursing Times!

Just before my contract ended, when we were due to return to England to get married, Phil decided that he would like to take me into the Congo (Zaire as it was then known). He wanted me to see where he hoped we would live after our marriage. Zaire was just recovering from the Simba rebellion civil war. Some areas were still held in rebel hands, including the area around Rethy where we were going. I managed to get a visa and a long weekend off. We travelled in 'Lucy' up to West Nile, then over the border at Goli. At the Zairian border post of Mahagi we found the rebels were still in control. At gunpoint they took away my passport, and I was very scared. To be left without your passport in a rebel area was terrifying. We prayed that I would be given it back on our return. For some reason they allowed Phil to keep his! Our destination, Rethy, was only twenty-five miles from the border. Some missionaries had returned after the war but only a few. They made us so welcome and were very excited to meet me. The African brethren were, too.

They exclaimed to Phil, "We knew you had a wife somewhere! Why didn't you bring her when you lived here?"

They could never understand that a man might not be married; it was inconceivable in their culture.

I was shown the bungalow which Phil had started to build, and although it had been partially wrecked by the rebels, the missionaries were gradually renovating houses and promised it would be finished for us in due course.

We spent a happy weekend there, and as much as I could I tried not to worry about my passport. Our last evening, all the missionaries gathered together for a banquet in our honour. They gave me a bouquet made not of real flowers but folded Ugandan banknotes tied onto twigs. It was an engagement present, and I was deeply moved at the generosity. We bought a pressure cooker with the money, and it was a blessing to us for many, many years!

I was sad to leave Uganda at the end of my contract. I had made many friends and learnt so much. There had been some difficult moments but also times of great joy. The sadness of the farewells was made bearable by the thought that Phil and I hoped to return to Africa after a year or so and, of course, by our impending marriage!

Marriage and Family

June 15th 1967 was the memorable day when Phil and I returned to England together. It was my father's birthday, and he and Mother had come to Heathrow airport to meet us. There was so much to tell them! It was also their first opportunity to really talk to Phil as our telephone conversations had been extremely brief due to cost. Although we had flown all night and slept very little, somehow the excitement of coming home kept me awake enough to greet my future in-laws when we finally arrived at Bath. They too gave me a kind welcome.

Our wedding had been planned for the following September, and the intervening months were busy not only with preparations but also with visits to churches to talk about Africa and visits to the Africa Inland Mission for me to be interviewed as a missionary candidate. Fortunately I had completed my Bible College Diploma with honours whilst in Uganda so did not need to go for further training.

Our wedding day came at last! I had three special people as bridesmaids: Joy; my UCH friend, Sylvia, who had by then also finished her contract in Uganda; and my young cousin, Shirley.

I had sewn my wedding dress by hand before I left Kampala and bought the material for the bridesmaids' dresses to match. My mother had worked so hard to prepare the reception, which was held in our church hall. We had two hundred guests, several of them missionary friends from Uganda. My friend Jennifer and her husband Graham were unable to attend because they were working in Iran, but Jennifer lent me her veil to wear. It was my 'something borrowed'!

After our wedding I needed to work to supplement our meagre allowance. I was able to get a job as a staff nurse at the Royal National Hospital for Rheumatic Diseases in Bath. It was a unique hospital with an interesting history and a great reputation in the field of rheumatology.

I enjoyed working there, but alas my stay was not to be for long. I soon became pregnant and seemed likely to miscarry my baby. As the work entailed a lot of lifting heavy, immobile patients, sadly it was agreed that I should leave. All the disappointment was soon forgotten once our first child, Mark, was born. Although he had been born three weeks before his due date, he was strong and bonny. A small problem was noted with Mark's spine before we left the hospital, and we had to take him to the children's hospital in Bristol to have it investigated. Although the visit revealed there was nothing of significance wrong with his spine, the investigations showed a heart defect! We were very dismayed and for a while it seemed that we would not be able to take Mark to Africa. Our close friends and family prayed with us, and the Lord answered in a wonderful way. When Mark was four months old we were told that the heart condition was resolving, and we could return to Zaire.

The Mission had expected that it would take quite a while for visas to be granted for us to return to Zaire (Congo) so Phil was advised to continue working in his part time job in a restaurant. Then suddenly we were told to pack and be ready to fly out in two weeks as our visas had arrived! It was a mad rush to get everything together! How much toothpaste and how many toilet rolls did I need to buy for the family for the next four years?

Phil went to Bristol docks and obtained some oil drums in which to pack our personal belongings. We also had a crate made for large items like the ironing board and Mark's pushchair. There was a rapid round of farewell meetings in our churches and goodbye meals with family and friends. My mother was extremely angry with me. As far as she was concerned I was taking her only grandchild into the jungle to be killed! As a grandmother myself I now understand far more how great the wrench must have been for her and Dad to see us go to a third world country where there had been war.

What a blessing it was that we had a placid baby! Mark coped with all the changes in his routine and environment without any problems. He slept all night in the plane between London and Uganda. We were to stay with missionaries near Kampala until such time as a missionary with a large enough vehicle could take us into Zaire. The missionaries with whom we stayed were friends of mine, and it was lovely to stay with them. We also were able to see the Holms' family. They all made such a fuss of Mark - I thought he would be spoilt forever!

We had been told by the Mission Council that we were to work in the very north of Zaire in an area called Zandeland. It was on the border shared with the Central African Republic and was very hot and dry. Phil had been designated to do youth work, and I was to run a dispensary. Neither of us had been very happy about this assignment. We had requested to return to Rethy, where Phil had lived and worked before the rebellion. He knew the language and understood the culture there. In those days missionaries had little choice about where they were sent so we had reluctantly agreed. One of our main concerns was that we would be living in such a remote place without any transport.

After a couple of weeks a car was found to take us into Zaire, as far as Rethy. We were told to wait there until someone could eventually transport us to Zandeland. We were taken by a missionary couple who were known to Phil. They were very kind. The journey took about five hours. It was hot and dusty, and we were all tired by the time we arrived at the border post. The border officials were drunk and not willing to let us through. Phil and our missionary driver got out to show all our papers and plead with them. Meanwhile, my usually placid baby decided to wail! The car was surrounded by African women and children who had never seen a white baby. They all wanted to touch him. I tried to feed him, but Mark was not going to be pacified! The African women were distressed for him; they went to the guards and told them they should let us through quickly because the 'muzungu' child was in pain!

Africans love children, and even the hearts of those drunken men were moved. Our papers were duly stamped, and we were allowed on our way. As soon as we were moving again, Mark fell asleep!

By the time we reached our destination the sun was setting rapidly (as it does near the equator). We were thankful to arrive before the darkness fell. Rethy was a big mission station with a large group of American missionaries working there. We were welcomed by the station manager and his wife, an older couple whose family had all 'flown the nest'. They had offered to give us hospitality while we were in transit.

Soon we were sitting down, having a very welcome drink, when we heard "Hodi!" called out. This is the traditional greeting: "May I come in?"

"Karibu!" our hosts responded. "Welcome!"

In walked Carolyn, the nurse in charge of the hospital. I had stayed in her home when I visited for the weekend before we left Uganda to get married. I thought she had just come to greet us and welcome us back to Zaire, but I was wrong.

"Hi! I am so glad to see you!" she said. "I have just received a message from the station at Linga where they have a shortwave radio. My father has had a severe stroke, and I need to go back to USA at once. Can you move into my house and take care of the hospital while I am gone?"

I was stunned and speechless. Take over the hospital? I had not studied for tropical medicine or gained my 'stage' needed by the government. I knew very little Swahili and had forgotten my 'O' level French. How would I manage?

Our host, the station manager, spoke for us!

"Excellent idea!" said Harry. "God's wonderful timing!"

Phil and I looked at each other. It didn't seem very wonderful to me! Yet we had prayed about staying at Rethy and given our plans to the Lord.

"Phil, you can take over the bookstore and printing press while you are here. There has been no-one to run it since you left four years ago."

Harry was quite excited by now!

"Maybe you will get the press up and running again before you have to go to Zandeland!"

"I'll call for you in the morning," Carolyn explained. "I will give you a tour of the hospital and my house. I expect to leave the day after and will be at home for at least three months. The nurses will help you look after little Mark while you are working. They will love him!" she added.

I didn't want anyone looking after my baby. I felt more and more miserable.

Things got even worse when Dorothy, Harry's wife, chipped in. "Your skirts are too short," she said, looking disapprovingly at my hemline (which, I might add, was not 'mini' as was the fashion but well below my knees!) "You can lengthen them in the morning while Phil goes with Harry to register you at the local government headquarters."

I tried to swallow back my tears and agree to her suggestion. Maybe it would be better when we were away from civilisation in Zandeland!

A good night's sleep does wonders, and the next morning I asked the Lord for grace, humility, patience and wisdom. I was here to serve the people, and if they would be offended by my skirts then I would lengthen them. If I was to work at the hospital then he would help me to cope one way or another.

What a blessing Mark was! He never fussed about being in different places or meeting different people. So long as he was fed at regular intervals and had lots of cuddles, he was happy.

Phil left with all our documents soon after breakfast while I bathed and dressed Mark. Then Carolyn arrived to give me the hospital tour. It was a complex of old buildings: a block for general patients that housed sixty beds, then another block of twenty maternity beds. There were buildings where relatives stayed and numerous cooking fires where they prepared food for their relatives. People were everywhere! Some were queuing patiently to see the nurse in the Outpatient's Clinic, others for blood tests and others for medicines. I accompanied Carolyn as she did her ward rounds. She told me about the patients, some with diseases I had never heard of.

Sometimes there were two people to a bed. In some wards people were sleeping on the floor under the beds as well. Were they patients or were they relatives? I wasn't sure.

The tour continued, and I was introduced to Nazan, the head nurse. He welcomed me warmly, speaking a little English. As the weeks went by I grew to appreciate Nazan so much. I grew to rely on his medical judgement and would never have survived the coming months without him. I also met Alice, the nurse who was in charge of the pharmacy. She made many ointments and lotions and even IV solutions herself. She was also in charge of all the sterilizing, which took place in large, old-fashioned autoclaves, heated by wood fires.

By the time we walked around the maternity wards and I met the pupil midwives, my head was spinning and I felt so inadequate. Nothing in my training had prepared me for this!

Then came the tour of Carolyn's house, which was next to the hospital. I met her 'boys' who helped with the cooking and cleaning. They were going to stay and help me, and when I saw the wood stove I knew I needed them! Perhaps I would have felt more positive if I had been given time to gradually get used to everything. As it was, I was really 'thrown in at the deep end' and felt as if I was drowning.

For some reason Carolyn had every confidence in my ability to cope.

"You British nurses are so well trained - and to be a midwife, too! That's something we Americans know little about!" she exclaimed.

Once the tour was over I had to look at my dresses. Dorothy allowed a couple to pass, but I had to set to work on the others. I was so glad when Phil returned and we could make plans about moving into the hospital house the next day. We had very little with us, just the bare essentials to keep us going until our freight arrived. We did have a few household items stored in West Nile, Uganda, which we had left before we went back to UK to get married. Phil thought he would try to borrow a vehicle to collect those before too long. There were no shops in the area, and we would need supplies of things like sugar and flour. Sometimes a lorry came through Rethy and sold such items to the missionaries, but all the other missionaries had cars or trucks and made frequent trips over the border to shop in Uganda. Our American colleagues told us to buy a vehicle, but we had no money and our allowances were far less than theirs so we couldn't see that happening.

Rethy Hospital

My introduction to Rethy Hospital had been very sketchy, but I was soon to learn by hard experience. We moved into Carolyn's house the day she left for the USA. After supper, on our first evening, I bathed and put Mark to bed, and Phil and I settled down to relax. The past few days had been physically and mentally exhausting. We were enjoying a truly British treat - a cup of tea - when there was a timid knock at the door. It was followed by the usual greeting.

"Hodi?" (May I come in?)

We answered, "Karibu!" (You are welcome), and in walked a student midwife.

"Mama," she said in the Kingwana language, "can you come to the maternity; we have a mother with the baby's arm hanging out."

Phil translated for me.

I questioned him, "Was that *really* what she said?"

My heart sank. An arm presentation! I had heard of such a thing but never seen one.

"Please, send someone to sit with our baby, and I will go and change," I found myself answering, trying not to show the panic I felt. Phil translated and the girl left. It was dark by now so Phil said he would first of all get the generator started and then come with me to help with language.

I quickly changed into my uniform and grabbed my trusted midwifery textbook, 'Maggie Myles'. I took a kerosene lamp from the hook and was lighting it when there was another knock at the door. I could say, "Karibu," to invite the person in but that was about all, so was pleased to see Phil arrive back to escort me to the maternity block.

I thought the young nurse had come to sit with Mark, but no; she had come to inform me there was a mother with an arm presentation. Phil told her that I already knew and was on my way.

"No, Bwana," she explained, "this is *another* arm presentation!"

What an introduction to midwifery in that part of Africa! I will never forget that night. We prayed over the first mother, and then I tried to push back the arm and turn the baby so that I could deliver it as a breech. We knew the baby had already died, and sadly it was the same with the second delivery. Both mothers did survive, but it had been a terrible experience for all of us.

That evening was the beginning of three very difficult months. There were more abnormal deliveries during that time than there had been for years. I know the Lord was teaching me to trust him and depend on his help. I was far away from my 'comfort zone' and dealing with conditions I had never even heard of. Often I was not able to contact any doctor for advice, and Nazan, helpful although he was, was not trained in midwifery. Our pupils and even trained midwives were not allowed to undertake abnormal deliveries.

The women around Rethy rarely came for antenatal care. It was the tribal custom to deliver the baby on the floor of your mother-in-law's hut. Should a woman fail to do this, it was a very bad omen for her. There was a lot of superstition and animistic belief and a great fear of being cursed. However, the women physically had very small pelvic bones, and this often made delivery very difficult. I saw so many women with dead babies due to obstructed labour which could have been prevented if they had come to the hospital for antenatal care or even early in their labour.

Within the first week I was called one afternoon to such a woman. I was thankful it was in daylight hours because Phil was able to speak to the duty doctor at Nyankunde Hospital, our main hospital which was about one hundred kilometres away. He told me to perform a symphesiotomy.

Whatever was that? I had no idea, except that it must be something to do with the symphysis pubic bone. Phil ran back to the radio shack and asked for instructions, and the nurses prepared a tray of instruments. I was told to anaesthetise the woman. Phil stayed and prayed with me before I began. The only way available to do this was to use a mask and an ether drip. I was scared stiff, but mercifully the patient became unconscious. Then I began to operate, with a trembling hand and racing heart, cutting through the cartilage of the symphysis pubis. All seemed well until the blade snapped off the scalpel handle. I sent Phil scurrying back to the radio because I had no idea what to do.

"The nurses should have known better and given you a solid blade scalpel," was the comment by the doctor. "Don't worry. The blade will embed itself in fat and not cause any harm. Ask for a solid scalpel and continue."

Meanwhile I had needed to top up the anaesthetic. I seemed to be running from one end of the patient to the other. (In due course I taught Phil how to help with anaesthetics.) Eventually I managed to cut through the cartilage and extract the dead baby. The mother recovered though I learnt afterwards that these patients needed to have an intravenous drip put up first. The doctor had forgotten to tell me that, or maybe he took it for granted that I would do so.

It was very painful for the mother to walk after this operation for some months, but it did mean that she should be able to deliver another child without problems. That particular patient gave birth to a live child about eighteen months later, and I was so delighted to see her. The scalpel blade had indeed become embedded in fat and caused her no problem!

It was always a blessing for me when the emergency arose during the day and we could have contact with a doctor, so long as there were no thunderstorms to interfere with the radio reception. Many of the patients held Phil in great awe, and because he kept coming to me with directions they thought he must be a doctor! It gave them great confidence!

Sometimes Nazan, the head nurse, was available to help with emergencies other than obstetric. His expertise was such a comfort to me. He always felt he should call me to look at any emergency in the general hospital before he made a decision. He called me one day to see a man with an enormous inguinal hernia. He politely asked me if I would like to try to push it back into place! I equally politely said I thought he could manage it without my help. He leaned over the patient and exerted his not inconsiderable strength, managing to reduce the hernia eventually. Then we decided that the patient should be driven down to Nyankunde hospital in our Volkswagen Kombi ambulance.

"Would Mama like to drive?" I was asked.

"Oh, Nazan! You know I have to drive in a circle all around the mission station because I cannot put the lever into reverse gear!" I replied. "Mama would *not* like to drive to Nyankunde!"

Nazan laughed. He went around the station and found another missionary who was happy to drive the patient for us.

Once a month, one of the doctors came from the hospital to visit us for a few days. We usually had a long list of patients for him to see, and among them were a lot who needed surgery.

I normally spent that week helping with anaesthesia while Nazan helped the doctor with actual operations. They were often very long and tiring days in the little theatre. I found it hard to leave Mark for so long, but Phil took him in his little pram down to the bookstore or the press.

Sometimes a lovely young girl called Kezia took him for a walk. On the station was a school for missionary children, and Kezia sometimes took Mark up to play with the baby daughter of one of the dorm parents there. I felt guilty about not spending more time with him during those first three months at Rethy, but he always seemed happy and contented.

One day we had an emergency when the patient needed a caesarean section. We had no doctor with us, and when we called Nyankunde on the radio they said the MAF (Mission Aviation Fellowship) plane had taken off to another emergency and no doctor was available to help. The woman's placenta was lying over the neck of the womb and beginning to bleed extensively so that her life was in danger. I called Nazan to help. We were both very nervous about operating but felt we had no choice. We prayed together, and Nazan began to give the spinal anaesthetic while I scrubbed up. Then we heard a screech of brakes as a car came to a halt outside the hospital. One of the student nurses called out that a white lady had come.

"Find out who she is and what she has come for," I said.

The nurse ran back with the news.

"Dactari Roseveare from Nyankunde!" she exclaimed.

"Bring her to us at once," Nazan called in Kingwana. "We need her help!"

A very reluctant Helen Roseveare was brought into the operating theatre, just in time to save the woman's life. Helen was reluctant because she taught medicine and did not undertake surgery. However, she was a doctor and we needed her!

Afterwards, when the emergency was over and we had thanked God, Helen explained that she had the distinct impression that she should call in at our station. Normally Helen drove all the way from Uganda to

Nyankunde without stopping, but how we thank God that she obeyed the 'still small voice' and drove into Rethy that day!

A short while after this, a young Irish doctor and his wife came to our station for three months for language study. John and Val Kyle were with the UFM (Unevangelised Fields Mission). Although John was not assigned to work at the hospital, he was wonderfully kind and willingly helped us when we had a dire emergency like a caesarean section.

Another challenge to me when I was left in charge of Rethy Hospital was the 'Monday Morning Clinic'. This was held in a small cottage near the hospital and was for Mzungus (the white population). Not only was there a considerable missionary population at Rethy, but also there were some Greek traders at the border post at Mahagi and a closed order of praying nuns from Belgium. The children at the mission school had their own nurse, Ellen Brown, who looked after their health.

I never knew who would turn up at that clinic. There was one senior missionary who made a habit of accosting me just after the service on a Sunday and telling me all about his haemorrhoids. I got fed up with asking him to come on a Monday to the clinic. He always claimed he was too busy for that! Eventually I referred him to the visiting doctor, explaining the situation. I don't know what he said to him, but he never troubled me at church again with his medical complaint.

The nuns from a nearby convent always came in their droves! Every Monday there would be a group of them, and they only spoke French. My problem was that they would not, or were not allowed to, speak for themselves, so one sister would relate the symptoms of another nun. They all jabbered like little birds let loose from their cage! It took ages to try and sort out what was wrong and how to help. I am sure they just loved this diversion from their lives of silence! Fortunately, in spite of my appalling French, most of the complaints were understood and the remedies seemed to work.

During the three months when Carolyn was away, I think I learnt more than in all my three years of training. I was so glad to see her come back!

Life Settles Down

One day we received a message that our freight had arrived at the Mahagi border crossing. I was so excited! It would be such fun unpacking our personal belongings. Mark needed larger clothes and some of the toys we had packed as well as having long outgrown the carrycot we had brought out from England. Phil was given permission to drive the mission station truck and collect the barrels and the crate. It was difficult to concentrate on my work that day, and every time I heard a vehicle on the dirt road outside the hospital I looked to see if Phil had returned.

Imagine what it felt like when he *did* arrive. I could see by his face that something was amiss. Yet there were the oil drums and the crate on the back of the truck. He didn't know how to tell me that the drums had been pilfered and were all so light they must be almost empty. How people had managed to get into them through the bunghole and then levering off the top we shall never know, but almost empty they were! I couldn't contain my disappointment. The tears just welled up in my eyes and spilled over. Our house helper lifted off the drums, looking at me and not knowing what to say. Fortunately the crate was intact, and we were thankful for that.

The bush telegraph spread the news like wildfire around that station, and it was the first of several times when we were touched by the caring attitude and love of our fellow missionaries and national friends. Some just came to sit with us and say they were sorry. Others asked us what we needed and prayed with us. It was the 'doctor's week' at the hospital and Dr Atkinson had brought his wife, Freda, with him as they had children in the academy and it was a chance for her to see them. She came rushing down from the school compound to be with me. I shall never forget what she said.

"Mary, dear, I know it is very hard, but in one way it makes you very much one of us. All of us missionary wives lost everything during the rebellion. We know how you feel and how hard it is today for you, but we will help you through this problem."

Freda was so loving and just like a mother to me that day. Indeed, the mission family did help us. No one else had a baby boy, but soon little trousers and tops began to arrive, along with toy cars and trucks. Mark certainly didn't miss out.

However, we did have a problem. News had reached us of Carolyn's imminent return, and we would need to vacate her home. We had our few belongings which we had stored in West Nile, Uganda, but very little else to equip our own house.

The Field Council met one day around that time at Rethy, and they, along with the local Church Council, had decided that we should not be sent up to Zandeland but stay at Rethy - Phil to continue with his bookstore and printing press assignment and I to work part time at the hospital, assisting Carolyn on her return. They had asked the missionary responsible for maintenance at Rethy to complete the bungalow which Phil had been building before the rebellion so that we could move there.

A local carpenter worked very hard and produced the basic furniture we would need, including a cot for Mark. Other missionaries produced unwanted curtains and we vacated Carolyn's house and moved in. Rethy is up in the rift valley, seven thousand feet above sea level, and can be cold, especially in the rainy seasons. That first evening, Phil had lit a fire in the living room, and we were sitting in front of it on a little mat, for as yet we had no chairs or table. Although it was dark, I had not yet pulled the curtains, and I saw a string of lights along the road. It was strange, and I wondered what was going on.

Then we heard, "Hodi?"

"Oh no!" I thought to myself. "Don't let it be another emergency at maternity!"

I sighed as I called out, "Karibu!"

To my amazement, the string of lights was a crocodile of missionaries carrying kerosene lamps. The first one had a folding table and came in and put it up. He was followed by people with chairs, table cloths, cutlery and crockery, and dishes of food! The station had decided to give us a housewarming party. They had thought of everything. And each family also brought us a gift. Their love made me cry! The gifts were so practical. One person had made a scraper to go outside our front door. It was a baked bean can, opened up and held by two thick sticks. He hammered it into the ground by the front step - such a practical gift and so useful in the rainy season when our shoes were muddy. I still have some of those gifts in my home forty years on!

By the time Carolyn returned we had more or less settled into our bungalow. She kindly allowed us to continue having one of her house helpers to work part time for us. Fanwelli was such a reliable help and adored Mark, so we were very grateful. Keziah continued to take him for walks when both of us were busy working.

We needed to have house help because it required so much labour to do everything by hand. We had no labour-saving devices. Our American friends had washing machines, but we didn't like to take up their offer for us to use them unless we were really desperate. Our helper washed our clothes and linen by hand, but once it was on the line, Keziah would sit outside to watch it. Washing had a way of vanishing into thin air and sometimes appearing in strange places! We had an older lady, Burnetta, who lived next door on one side of us. One day she had all her 'smalls' disappear off her line. Well, she was quite large so they were not exactly small 'smalls'! Included among her laundry was an old-fashioned corset - totally irreplaceable in Zaire. She was distressed about the loss of this item, but it didn't help matters when a man arrived in church on Sunday morning adorned in her corset, neatly clipped together over his trousers! It was terribly hard not to giggle all through that service. No doubt he had bought it in the local market and thought it a splendid garment for Sunday wear!

I didn't have to do so many night calls once Carolyn was back, but I did take my turn to make life easier for her. I also took over the oversight of the pharmacy. I enjoyed making the ointments and lotions as well as preparing the intravenous solutions, working alongside Alice, a competent nurse. Another duty, which really stretched me, was to teach some midwifery and baby care to the pupil midwives. I needed to prepare the lessons in English and then translate them into French. However, many of the students did not have a good working knowledge of French so the discussion in the classroom was usually in Swahili. My knowledge of both languages was minimal! I went to Congo Swahili (Kingwana) classes each week, taught by a dear older lady missionary called Annie. She was extremely patient with me. Often I had Mark in a pushchair. He was not always quiet, and also by this time I was pregnant again and often tired.

My practical assignments were to teach child development to the women who came to our mothers' class on a Wednesday afternoon. I also ended each session with a flannel graph lesson on the book of Esther. We had such fun with this, and I have loved the book of Esther ever since!

Mark was a great model for the child development class! Many of the mothers could not be persuaded to supplement their breast milk by introducing other foods into their children's diets before they were two years old. I used to mash up bananas and feed them to Mark, and he would demonstrate that babies liked being weaned and God had given them teeth to use! My rosy-cheeked, fair-haired, happy baby delighted his audience and was living proof that it was good to give babies solid food once they had begun to get their teeth.

I did enjoy teaching health education to these women. I had no idea then that in retirement I would have the opportunity to go back to Africa to continue that kind of work or, indeed, that health education in one form or another would play such a major part in my career.

For my final language examination I had to teach a class of teenagers a Bible story. Somehow those teenagers were scarier than the mother's group, but with God's help I managed! I was so delighted when I had finished my language study but, even so, was still far from fluent in the vernacular. It never ceased to amaze me that once Mark had begun to talk he could speak in several languages to people. He always seemed to know who would understand which one!

There were times when food was a problem for us. We had a very small kerosene fridge with just a tiny freezing compartment, so on the occasions when the local butcher killed a cow, although meat was available, we could only store very little. This butcher had a 'soft spot' for Mark, and knowing the British liked liver he would often present us with the liver as a gift. That was such a treat!

When I was in the early months of pregnancy we were particularly short of protein for some reason. I heard a knock at the door one morning and the usual "Hodi?" called out.

I went to see who was there, and three of the local school teacher's wives were outside. I met with these wives each week for Bible study and also craft work. They were dear friends.

That morning they had brought me some eggs. I knew that everyone was short of food at that time, and I found it hard to accept their sacrificial gift.

"Madame, you need them for your growing baby," they said.

"But you need them too," I answered.

"You should know, Madame, that if we African women eat eggs, they make us infertile, but it is alright for you Muzungu women!"

I never succeeded in expelling this myth from their minds. If the women had only eaten eggs then their general health might have been better.

After we had been in Zaire for about a year we were able to get away for a short holiday. Carolyn had lent us her van and we planned to go to Uganda to visit my spiritual parents, the Holms. It was rainy season and we left Rethy at first light in order to get through the border and on our way before it became too hot. It was raining - the sort of rain that comes like stair rods from heaven! We found that the van's windscreen wipers were not working, and it was really difficult to drive to the border. I was sitting in the small room at the border while Phil did the paperwork, when a toddler came into the room. He was smartly dressed in a Marks and Spencer's sailor suit such as I had packed in our freight for Mark. At least I knew where some of the pilfering of our freight had happened!

When we eventually arrived in Kampala in the late afternoon, it was to find a distressed Lynn waiting for us.

"Thank God you are here," he said, with great feeling.

"Whatever has happened?" I asked him.

"Brian fell off the garage roof this morning and is in hospital with a fractured skull. Can you look after the other children while I join Marcie? They need feeding."

"Of course," I answered. "Don't worry about the family; I will take care of them."

I knew the Holms' home very well because when I lived in Kampala I used to house-sit when they went away, as well as it being 'second home' to me.

Lynn departed, and Phil and I gathered Sherry, Lynette, Jonathan and Joel together. They told us all about the accident. The children had being playing ball. One throw shot the ball onto the roof of the garage and in spite of being told many times not to climb on its roof, Brian, the youngest, had done so. He had then thrown the ball down, overbalancing as he did so. Now the little five-year-old was dangerously ill in Mengo Hospital. The children were all naturally very upset, and we prayed with them. To distract them I suggested that they play games and amuse Mark while I made a meal for everyone. We spent that week looking after the four children, just seeing Lynn and Marcie for a few moments when they came home to rest. People all over the world were praying for Brian, and, praise God, he regained consciousness after a few days and then made a complete recovery. It hadn't exactly been the restful holiday we had anticipated, but how glad we were to be there to help our very close friends in their time of need. Marcie often spoke about it in following years, saying that I probably knew her children better than anyone else and that she was so happy that I was able to take over for that week. Phil managed to get the windscreen wipers fixed while we were in Kampala, and we did some much needed shopping before we drove back to Rethy.

One of the greatest excitements at Rethy was the day the plane flew in with the mail. Once a month, the MAF plane touched down on the little airstrip. As soon as its engine was heard flying above us, mission cars would drive out and also many local people ran out to see it. We Brits were often the envy of the station because our friends and family wrote so faithfully to us. We always had lots of mail. Sometimes it was a double-edged sword for me as reading the mail would make me homesick, especially for family. One day I recall feeling so homesick that I felt I had to get off the station. That day Rethy, instead of feeling like the centre of the universe, seemed like the end of the world! I put Mark into his pushchair and walked and walked along the mud tracks and villages near the station.

"Where are you going?" people called to me.

"I am just walking," I answered, trying to control the tears which kept streaming down my face. The villagers looked at me in astonishment. I am sure they wondered what these mad Mzungus would do next!

Missionaries do get bad days, just like anyone else. That day happened to be my mother's birthday; maybe that contributed to my homesickness.

Time to Leave

For every sad time there were many happy ones! There was always something to celebrate at Rethy. Each Saturday evening there was some sort of programme to entertain the children at the missionary academy. We had children as young as five years, through to around thirteen years, after which they transferred to the Rift Valley Academy in Kenya. It was always fun taking part in the activities and also thinking of different things we could do.

Birthdays were special times too. It never ceased to amaze me how creative people were when it came to presents! When Mark had his second birthday one of our friends, Paul Brown, made a set of wooden bricks in a very lightweight local wood, and his wife Ellen must have spent hours sanding them down. Those bricks were Mark's pride and joy for many years and were handed down to his brothers and sisters; they are still played with by the grandchildren today! Paul also made, at Carolyn's request, a swing for the garden. That as well was the source of much delight.

An elderly, retired missionary, a widower, returned to Rethy about this time. His name was Rev. Harry Stam. He came from Dutch American stock, and his brother had been a missionary in China. A book had been written about him: 'The triumph of John and Betty Stam'.

Harry became a daily visitor to our house every afternoon at teatime. He thought English teatime was the most civilized invention! He soon became 'Grandpa Stam' to Mark, and the two of them were very great friends. We enjoyed Harry's company so much. He also celebrated Christmas with us - as traditionally English as one could make it in the centre of Africa! Later on, when we had returned to UK he was a regular visitor to our home, stopping for a couple of weeks each time he came from or returned to Africa. Eventually he married Martha, a single missionary living in the next little house to us and also a dear friend. We were thrilled that they were able to spend the last years of their lives together.

Rethy was the largest of AIM's mission stations in Zaire at that time, and its school served missionaries of many denominations and societies, from several countries. This meant there were always a lot of 'comings and goings'. Frequently we entertained parents who were bringing or fetching children to school or visiting at half term. The half term was a long weekend, and children did not go home, but parents were always welcome. There were special activities like picnics, which were great fun. It meant that we were able to make many friends. Often there were station 'bring and share' dinners. I have such a clear memory of my son who became very impatient to start eating, and as a long 'grace' was being said (which included a blessing for all our guests) he started to bang his spoon on the highchair and shout, "Amen!" He knew 'amen' meant he could begin to eat!

During our first few months at Rethy I miscarried a pregnancy in its early weeks. A few months later, when I found I was pregnant again, we were delighted and excited. By this time Carolyn was back so my duties at the hospital lessened. Most of the time I kept reasonably well, and we were all looking forward to an addition to our family. Carolyn kindly was willing to monitor me through the antenatal period, and Dr. Ruth Dix had agreed to come from the main hospital at Nyankunde to deliver me, or alternatively I could go down there.

At the time, Phil and I were going through a time of testing. As a British couple our support level was far below our American and Canadian colleagues. We were becoming in debt to the mission treasurer. Just living took more than our allowance, and however careful we were we could not make ends meet.

At our annual mission field conference we were sharing with an American lady missionary who had recently been widowed. She had two teenage boys at R.V.A. in Kenya. Her husband had died from a heart attack, and before his death she had been unaware that he was worrying about the money he needed to pay their fees. When he died, she realised she was almost penniless. We shared with Jean our problems. Other than the Lord, and presumably the field treasurer, no one else was aware of our situation. We covenanted together that we would pray for six months, and if at the end of that time we were still in need we would take it that we were to return home.

We prayed earnestly through those months. At the end of the six months Jean's situation had changed dramatically, and she was in good financial health. For us, the situation became worse and worse! A hydro-electric scheme had been installed at Rethy to bring electricity to the whole station. We had no choice so we were all 'wired up' and a standing charge levied from all the mission staff. This monthly levy was more than our entire mission allowance for all three of us. And soon there was to be another child!

Phil went to talk things over with 'Mr. Money Bags', as the missionary children affectionately called Stanley Kline, the field treasurer. With great sadness, we then gave three months' notice and made plans to return to UK.

During that time, one Sunday morning, I felt 'twinges' and had a strange feeling that labour was about to start. I was only seven months pregnant. I stayed home from church. When Phil and Mark returned, the pains were increasing, so I sent for Carolyn to examine me. I was indeed in early labour.

Through that day she monitored me, hoping that maybe things would settle down. She talked to Dr. Ruth on the radio, who agreed to fly up the next day or sooner, if necessary.

The labour progressed, and I moved down to a small house near the hospital where we were to stay for the delivery and postnatal period. I wasn't unduly concerned because I had looked after so many premature infants, and Carolyn felt this baby was a good size for the dates.

Ruth arrived and examined me, and five o'clock that afternoon I was delivered of a baby girl, weighing four pounds and six ounces. We were thrilled with our tiny daughter, whom we called Alison Joy.

Perhaps that evening was one of the happiest we experienced. We introduced Mark to his new little sister, and we gave thanks to God together as we sat around the log fire in the tiny cottage. A few of our closest friends, missionary and Congolese, came to visit us. One of them, Larry Clements, a young Canadian, whose first baby I had delivered only weeks earlier, arrived with his camera. He wanted to take a family photo, but I was tired and asked him to wait until the next day. This was a decision I will regret to my dying day.

The nights could be cold at Rethy, especially at certain times of the year, so when Carolyn came in to check on us and say goodnight, she advised me to keep Alison beside me in the bed since she was so tiny. I am glad I did that, holding her close and suckling her from time to time through that night. Early the next morning, maybe about 6am, I was concerned about Alison's colour and breathing. I knew something was wrong and called for Phil, who was in the next room, sleeping with Mark. He went running over to Carolyn's house, and she came, along with Dr. Ruth, as quickly as she could.

Phil and I sat together, holding each other and praying as Ruth and Carolyn tried to help our baby. We watched her slip away into eternity with heavy hearts.

Life in the tropics brings its own problems. Phil had to rush to the local government centre to register Alison's birth before he could then register her death so that she could be buried.

There was no way that Ruth could do an autopsy, and because of the climate she had to be buried that afternoon. Ruth had put on the death certificate what she felt sure had been the cause of death: hyaline membrane disease. This is a condition which occurs in premature babies due to immaturity of their lungs. The fact that Alison was a good weight belied the fact that she was very premature. We had no incubators or resuscitation equipment or oxygen available. Later my young brother, Tim, was to send a simple resuscitation mask to help the hospital, in memory of his niece.

I was allowed to dress and was driven to the small missionary cemetery for her burial. Carolyn had chosen the prettiest baby dress from my layette and wrapped her in a shawl. Paul Brown, our dear friend, had that morning made a little coffin, and Burnetta, our neighbour, who was wonderful at growing flowers, had covered the top with a beautiful arrangement. Our dear Congolese pastor gave a message of encouragement and hope, though I was too shocked to appreciate it. All I remember of that service was singing the old hymn 'It is well; it is well with my soul'.

By the time I was taken back to the little house I was feeling confused and shocked and also full of abdominal pain. People kept coming to sit with me, but I wanted to be left alone, even though I know they came with love in their hearts. MAF had flown Dr. Ruth back to Nyankunde, and so it was just Carolyn who came to check on me in the early evening. I was burning up with fever and in a lot of pain. All the usual checks were done in case I had a bout of malaria, and in the end, because I was delirious, she felt she had to do a 'D&C' operation to make sure I had no piece of placenta left behind in the womb. Poor Carolyn! She felt I was too sick to take an anaesthetic and so just did what she could without one. There is little I remember of the next day or so, except a vision or clear spiritual picture. I don't know what it was, but I saw Jesus carrying my baby in his arms. I knew without a doubt she was safe with the Lord. I had many questions and many struggles in the weeks that lay ahead, but I never doubted that Alison was with the Lord. I needed that reassurance; as a young Christian I had been in a group discussing salvation, and the minister leading had said that he could not give assurance to any mother whose baby had died because the scriptures say, "We are conceived in sin from our mother's womb."

With antibiotics I gradually recovered. I did not appreciate how sick I had been until Phil one day remarked that he thought he was to lose his wife as well as his child. As soon as I was well we had to pack up and return to England. I felt as if it was all too much to cope with. For Mark's sake I tried to keep things as normal as possible, but inside I felt like screaming! One dear single lady missionary on a nearby station invited me and Mark to go to her home for a week. We drove over, and she ministered to me with love and kindness, and I rested. Then we moved in with our Canadian friends, the Clements, for the final few days while we sold almost everything we owned to pay off our debts. With just one small trunk containing our most precious things we left Zaire and went to Kampala to stay with Lynn and Marcie for a day or so before flying home.

Before we left Rethy the mail had arrived. Inside was an advert for a bookshop manager in the Scripture Union bookshop in Croydon. One of my nursery flat mates, Jeannette, had married an Anglican minister, Rev. Garry Guinness. They were faithful prayer partners and when they knew we were returning to England they sent out this advert and also talked to folk in Scripture Union about us. When we arrived in Kampala there was another letter also containing the same advert. God had not abandoned us but rather gone before!

Mary with her older brother, John, aged 4 years. 1945.

Top left: *First day of training at University College Hospital, London.*
Top right: *UCH Nurses' Home.*
Bottom right: *Presentation of gold medal by Lady Reading. 1964.*
Bottom left: *Bradford-on-Avon hospital – pupil midwife. 1965.*

Top left: 1967 with a young patient at the
Infant Malnutrition Research Centre in Kampala, Uganda.
Top right: Marriage to Philip Weeks. 1967.
Bottom: Africa Inland Mission Hospital at Rethy,
Democratic Republic of the Congo. 1968-1970.

Top left: *Phil and Mary with Mark, Paul and Jennifer. 1973.*
Top right: *Mary's marriage to Rev. Malcolm Millard. April 2006.*
Bottom: *Rwanda – Health Education Project*
to raise awareness of family planning.

4

School Nursing

Starting Life in Croydon

*W*e travelled back to England in a VC10 aircraft on a night flight. What a sorry sight we were when we embarked from the plane! Mark had been sick several times. His little suit was stained and smelly. I had hardly dozed and was so weary. Poor Phil was trying to cheer us both up and gather the luggage etc. What our families thought when they saw us, I shall never know! Mark was terrified by all the noise of the London traffic. He had lived almost all this life in the bush and had only seen a few cars or trucks. He kept pointing to vehicles but then putting his hands over his ears because of the noise!

Phil's brother, Gordon, and his wife, had hired a mini bus and brought our parents up to Heathrow to meet us. We stopped at a park for a picnic, and my mother produced a little Matchbox car for Mark, which he held onto all the way home to Bath. For him, Granny and Granddad were just names, and England wasn't home as it was to us. On our first Sunday we attended our sending church, Widcombe Baptist. It is a large and well-attended church. We took Mark up to the balcony and sat down in the front row.

He peered over the rail and asked in a loud voice, "Are all these my uncles and aunties?"

Almost every face was white, and all Mzungus had been adopted uncles and aunties to him. He was quite bewildered! I was bewildered too when I went shopping. The aisles in the supermarket had so much choice I found it hard to make decisions and would come out without buying anything!

We stayed with my parents for a few months. It wasn't an easy time for any of us. There was the baby for whom we were all grieving; I had a uterine infection that was troublesome; Mark developed pneumonia and also amoebic dysentery; Phil was job-hunting, then working at a bookstore in Bristol; and we were also house/flat-hunting with no success at all.

Phil had wanted to stay in the Bath area because he longed to serve in Widcombe Baptist Church which had supported us so lovingly while we were away. However, jobs and housing were not working out. For three months we struggled, and all this time Scripture Union were headhunting him for the post in Croydon about which we had been told before we left Zaire. Finally, we got the message! Maybe the Lord wanted us there!

Phil went to Croydon for an interview, and then they asked me to go up as well. Although I would not be working with Scripture Union, they wanted to be sure that I would be happy to live in Croydon and support Phil in his work. I must admit that I was surprised that they cared so much about the whole family. Even though I was very unimpressed by what to me seemed a real concrete jungle, I was prepared to go wherever the Lord led us. By now it was obvious that we needed to move from my parents' home as soon as possible to give them their space again.

Phil was appointed to the position of manager of the Croydon SU bookshop and overall manager of the other bookshops in their chain. (The chain later grew to such an extent that it had to be divided into northern and southern areas, and Phil continued to look after the southern shops.)

He stayed temporarily with some friends, and leaving Mark with my parents, I joined him for a week in order to house-hunt. How different it is when you are in God's plan! While Phil was at work, my hostess took me to an estate agent to pick up details of affordable houses in the area. We had very little money and no idea if we could buy anything. Only one or two seemed to be suitable, and that very evening we went to look at the outside of them. We were not sure about the location of the first one; the second one was a small terraced house and looked just right. The price had been reduced that very day for a quick sale, and on the details it said, "Viewing by arrangement with the owner." This emboldened us to knock on the door, and an elderly gentleman welcomed us in and allowed us to view the property. He wanted to sell quickly and move to be with his daughter. The house seemed to welcome us, even though it was in dire need of cleaning up!

Before we went back to Bath that weekend SU had helped us by having it surveyed, and we were able to begin proceedings to buy it. Even now, I am not sure where the money came from for the deposit. I think I may have withdrawn my National Health superannuation; somehow the Lord provided.

We moved from Bath just after Christmas to South Croydon where we rented a house for three months before finally moving into our own home. My mother came to help us move because, against all medical predictions of infertility, I was once again pregnant. Our new house was filthy. My dear mother scrubbed away at the lino on the stairs and emptied bucket after bucket of black water. The ceiling of the dining room was dark brown and covered with blobs of nicotine. We had almost no furniture, but we had a home.

In the evenings Phil began to drive a van for the Missionary Mart in nearby Wallington. This charity collected unwanted household items, auctioned the best and sold the rest in their warehouse. It had been the brainchild of the parents of one of my UCH flatmates, Jeannette. The mart has raised literally millions of pounds over the years for mission. It helped us, too! Sometimes Phil would be asked to collect an item; it would be just what we needed for our home, and he was able to buy it. So gradually we furnished our home and settled down.

We also found a loving fellowship in Woodside Baptist Church. We soon made friends, and Mark had playmates. I missed Rethy so much and found it hard to live in such an urban setting. When, in October 1971, our second son was born at UCH, we so valued the support of our new church family as he was a very sick baby and needed to be nursed in the special care baby unit. I thought I was going to lose Paul too. I was grateful to be back at UCH where there was so much expertise and equipment available to help immature babies for he had been born four weeks early.

Eighteen months later, in April 1973, we had the gift of another child - our daughter, Jennifer. My time was now well occupied with caring for our little family, and we were growing out of our small house too. Those were years of financial hardship and difficulty but also very happy years as we nurtured the children. My ongoing gynaecological problems led to a prolonged stay in UCH with very major surgery, when once again family and friends came to our aid and took care of the children.

Through these years we were delighted that many of our missionary colleagues from Zaire as well as my spiritual mother and her family from Uganda came to stay with us.

It was always a challenge to sleep everyone but such a delight!

About nine months after my surgery I had a hormonal disturbance that sent me into an anxiety state. I thank God it was short-lived, but it was quite terrifying. My GP, a dear Christian friend who later became my employer, felt that where we lived was too isolated from most of our church family and friends. He suggested that we try to move from East Croydon to Addiscombe.

His suggestion planted a seed in my mind which was watered when I left the surgery and went to have a coffee with a friend in the Addiscombe area. This friend had recently moved from very near our house, where she had attended our small ladies' Bible study group and come to faith, to a larger home.

Out of the blue, while we were drinking coffee together, she said, "Mary, I do miss you. I wish you lived over here. I know a friend who is going to sell her house soon; it would be perfect for you. Why don't you go and have a look at it?"

I didn't like to say that there was no way we could afford to move to that area but agreed that I would talk to Phil about it.

The following weekend another UCH flatmate from The Nursery came to stay. Heather was engaged to be married to Dr. John Knowles, and they were preparing to go to the mission field. We had a lovely weekend catching up on all the news. After she had gone I talked to Phil about both our GP's and my friend's suggestions about moving. We prayed together. We did not want to miss hearing the Lord's voice because we felt it was financially a non-starter.

That week Heather wrote a note to thank us for our hospitality. She commented on how crowded we were in our small house and that maybe it was time to move. She also enclosed a cheque for £80.00, adding, "I know this is a very small amount, but it can start a fund for your move!"

In fact, it was a most generous gift and touched our hearts so much. Here was this young lady with a wedding to prepare for and a life of mission ahead, giving so sacrificially to us. We took that gift as a promise from the Lord that he would provide for us to move.

When we went to view the house which my friend had recommended, we were just overcome. It was so spacious and well-equipped. The kitchen was fitted and even had a washing machine. Up until that time I had not had such luxuries. It felt like home from the moment we walked through the front door. We sat and talked with the couple who were hoping to sell the house and move closer to the husband's work. They were not in a hurry to move as the house they hoped to buy would be a little while before it became available; so as yet they had not put their own home on the general market. We loved the house, but the price was far beyond our means. It would take a miracle to be able to buy it.

The months went by, and I tried to put that house out of my mind. It just seemed too perfect! We didn't look at any others. Eventually, the family were in a position to sell and gave us a first offer. We had prayed long and hard, and Phil felt that we should go forward in faith. In our church was a couple with one daughter who had emigrated from India. They could only get a mortgage for ten thousand pounds, and there was almost no property available for that price. The house we wanted was priced at thirteen thousand. How small those prices seem now, but then it was an enormous sum! As we prayed we felt that we should offer our house to this family and trust the Lord for the three thousand deficit. Phil went to visit the solicitor, and to my amazement he was willing to act on our behalf.

"You have told me the selling and the buying price," he commented. "I presume you have the money to make up the difference?" he asked.

"No," replied Phil, "we don't have it yet."

"Then I presume you know where it will come from?" he enquired.

"Well," answered Phil, "I don't, but my heavenly Father does!"

"That's alright then. I will go ahead and act for you," the solicitor agreed.

That was a miracle in itself, but we were to see the hand of God in an even more amazing way.

The weeks passed and we were about to sign the contract but still did not have the money.

I was struggling. Had we really been led out in faith or were we being presumptuous? Almost the day before we were due to complete the sale and purchase I went to the evening service at church while Phil stayed at home with the children. When I returned it was to find a car drawn up outside our house, and inside was a friend who attended another church. He had come alone; his wife was at home with her children. After a cup of tea and general chat, he told us the real reason for his visit.

"My wife and I have never given consistently to missionaries, and God has been speaking to us about that," he said, "so we thought about it and asked the Lord who we should support. Your names came at once to mind. We tried to think of overseas missionaries who needed money, but we just kept coming back to your names so have decided to support you. We were going to arrange a certain sum each month, but the Lord impressed upon us that you need help right now. We have heard you hope to move and we thought this might help."

He handed Phil a cheque for £2,000 and then another to me for £1,000.

"I have been to the tax office, and with the new gift tax regulations I understand that I can give the £2,000 to you and my wife can also give to Mary," he added.

We didn't know whether to laugh or cry. It was so amazing! The amount was exactly what we needed. It was so hard to even begin to thank this couple for their generosity. We later learnt that they had borrowed from one of their relatives in order to give us this large amount and had arranged to pay them back each month. What a sacrifice they made!

Very soon after this our church family helped us move into our new home, and our dear Indian friends moved into the small house. What a blessing it was to us all! Our new home in Addiscombe never ceased to be a joy to us, and we lived there for many years.

Finding Work

Once the children were all at school I began to wonder if I should go back to work. Finances were always very tight, and by now my husband had been diagnosed with a neurological illness. We did not know how long he would be able to work in a full time capacity. I began to pray and seek the Lord. Part of me hated the thought of not being at home for the children. Nursing posts usually entailed shift working, and that did not fit easily with family life.

One day a small, duplicated advert was put through the letterbox. It was asking for trained midwives to return to work because there was a great shortage in the area. I decided to make further enquiries and was duly asked to go to the Mayday Hospital in Croydon for an interview.

The nurse manager talked at length with me. I would need to do a refresher course, working full time for three months. After that I could work part time. I was asked if I would then be interested in working on the premature baby unit.

I certainly loved working with the 'premmies', and so the nurse manager decided to take me over to visit the unit. We were about to go when the phone rang. It was for me! I was stunned. The only person who knew I was having the interview was Phil. It was his assistant manager telling me that Phil had collapsed and had been taken to the casualty department at Mayday Hospital.

I explained to the midwife what had happened.

"Is there anyone I can call to go with you to casualty?" she asked.

I thought instantly of a dear friend who I knew from UCH days who was now working as a sister tutor at the Mayday.

"Can you possibly see if Beryl Sowden if free?" I asked.

"Of course," she answered and then added, "Don't worry about this interview. When things are settled at home, just phone me. I will always have a place here for you"

Beryl came with me and stayed until Phil had been seen. I told her why I had come to Mayday that morning. She also counselled me to forget all about going back to midwifery at the moment. Later that day Phil was allowed home, and we stopped *en route* and bought the local paper. During the weekend I was reading it when I noticed an advert from the school health department. They were looking for a school nurse to work school hours, term time only. It was also a sister's post so had a reasonable salary. As I read it, my heart leapt; this would be the perfect job! So I applied and was offered an interview. The job description was far wider than I had expected and included health education for the pupils. At the interview I learnt how progressive the department was, and the job would be a far cry from the 'nit nurse' image that school nurses had traditionally held. The only drawback was that the area where the nurse was needed was at the opposite end of the Croydon Borough from where we lived. That would mean I would have to arrange some sort of childcare before and after school for my children.

The week following the interview the nursing officer phoned me to say she was very sorry but I had not been offered the post. However, she asked if I could be kept on her books should another post become vacant. I had felt the Lord was showing me a career path that would fit in with the family and was confused at not getting the job. What was the Lord saying in all this? Looking back I think he was teaching me to trust him and wait for his timing to see the golden thread.

Not many weeks later I received another phone call from the School Health Department offering me a post as school nurse based in our local health centre, working in the area around our home. It was the perfect job for me and much better than the one I had originally been disappointed at not getting.

I did not need to make any arrangements for childcare. The boys were both at senior school and Jenny in her final year at primary. She was in the same school as the children of my closest friend, Jean, who kindly said she would bring Jenny home from school each day and that I could collect her from her house.

I began my new job on the first day of the January term, the year I was forty. It was a bad winter and even the London area was very icy and snowy. We had been given a little car by a close friend. It was a wonderful provision as I needed to be mobile for my work, but I wasn't used to driving in such conditions. The bad weather lasted that year for almost the whole term. I could drive in mud or on very dusty roads with ruts and bad cambers, but London in the ice and snow was very challenging!

At the health centre I shared the open office with two other school nurses and four health visitors. My 'patch' contained two high schools and five primary schools. It took a while to get to know the staff and pupils and to learn 'the ropes'. The other school nurses were very helpful, and in time we became good friends. School nurses were also expected to help the health visitors with the running of their baby clinics at least once a week so I got to know them quite well too. On the whole it was a good office to work in. At first it was not easy. One of my colleagues on the school nursing team was from the West Indies. Although she was a committed Christian, she had a big 'chip on her shoulder' about missionaries. In her opinion they had gone to the West Indies to steal their wealth under the pretext of sharing the Gospel. I didn't quite know how to answer her claims but just remarked that we certainly hadn't gained any wealth by our missionary years in Africa! Others in the office had some very negative experiences of Christians, but in time they came to accept and trust me. When my other school nursing colleague sadly went through a divorce, she and I spent a lot of time together, and she for a while was seeking to know the Lord, but I don't think she ever took the step of really committing her life to Jesus.

One of the senior schools where I worked was South Norwood High School. I was pleased to be allocated this school as I was leader at that time of the girl Covenanter Class at Woodside Baptist Church, and quite a number of the group were pupils there. It was good to see friendly faces around the campus, and at break times often the girls came in to visit me. Sadly the school was due to close at the end of the academic year so my time there was short.

The other senior school where I worked was Stanley Technical Boys' High School, also in South Norwood. It had been founded by Stanley of 'Stanley Tools' fame and was a flourishing institution at a time when technical schools were out of fashion and almost non-existent. My own boys were young teenagers at this time, and that did help me a little when getting to know my young clients. Most of them really were not interested in their own or the health of anyone else so it was hard work doing any form of health education.

Occasionally I would be asked to do a foot inspection. I needed a clothes peg for my nose. Can you imagine examining foot after sweaty foot to spot a verruca! It almost made me faint on a hot afternoon! However, I soon learnt that fainting was the forte of these teenage boys when they were given their final booster injections or BCG's! I have never known so many boys, often twice my size, turn a ghastly shade of green and slither to the floor after the insertion of a tiny needle! The school secretary, the duty doctor and I used to dread the injection clinic days at that school. A number of boys also managed to 'disappear' when it was their turn to come! Needle phobia was a very real and ever present disease!

When South Norwood High School was closed down I was allocated a private Convent School in Upper Norwood. It was called Virgo Fidelis and mostly staffed by nuns. It had a junior school as well, and so that was added to my workload. As much as possible I went each Friday and spent the morning at the junior school and afternoon at the senior school. I found that it was a completely different working environment to any of my other schools. At first I found the nuns extremely polite but quite distant. I felt they resented the intrusion of the school health service and that I was there on sufferance. Gradually over the months and years the atmosphere changed, and I began to look forward to my Fridays.

The headmistress of the junior school was a very interesting lady. She had been brought up in a Christian home, and her parents had attended the Baptist Church but had sent her to the local convent school for her education. When she was due to leave she had no idea what to do with her life. She told me she had drifted into being a nun rather than having any sense of calling. Then she had trained as a teacher and found her vocation. She loved her small pupils and they loved her! There was always a happy atmosphere in the classrooms and she was also very co-operative when I needed girls to come to the medical room for examination. One day she was chatting to me and learnt that I had worked in the Congo. She was very excited about this because the order to which the nuns belonged was a teaching order with one more school in England and also one in Congo. Then she invited me to talk to the girls about the Congo.

When my daughter, Jenny, was to be baptised by immersion at our own church, she expressed a desire to come and witness it. She remembered what joyful occasions baptisms had been in the church where she had grown up. That headmistress will also be remembered for all time by my own family because she gave them a gerbil out of a litter the school pet produced!

After the morning session was finished I made my way to the senior school. At one time it had been a boarding school and still boasted a sanatorium with about eight beds and two nuns to look after it! These nuns were nearing retirement but I think must have been a little frustrated by rarely having any pupils to look after. Occasionally a girl would be sent to them if she felt unwell for any reason while waiting for the parents to collect her.

These sisters looked after me as if I was their daughter. As soon as I arrived I was offered lunch. I started by taking out my sandwiches as usual, but after a week or so I realised they really did want me to have a proper lunch so I gave into them and ate what was, I must say, a pretty nice school lunch. The sanatorium was at the top of the school. The next floor down contained the now redundant dormitories, and on the ground floor were the classrooms and administration. I was never allowed to go to the ground floor! These two nuns loved to go to the classrooms and collect the girls I needed to see. They were always very discreet and disappeared once my client had arrived, allowing us to talk in privacy. Some of these girls, although from privileged backgrounds, did have problems. Very few were from a Catholic background but were all required to go to Chapel services each day. Many were from ethnic minority groups, whose parents preferred their daughters to attend a single sex school and one with high academic standards even though they often adhered to another religion.

Not long before I began working at this school, one of the girls became severely anorexic and died. Not so much was known about this tragic condition in 1970-80's, and the school wanted to be sure that such a thing never occurred again. Because of this, there was a great emphasis on good nutrition, and I was asked to counsel the girls on a one-to-one basis. I found that very satisfying.

The days when we had an immunisation clinic or general medicals the nuns set up the sanatorium like a hospital, with beds screened and a general smell of antiseptic everywhere. I think it must have reminded them of 'the good old days' because they bustled around, humming under their breath. We were supplied with coffee and biscuits or tea and cakes at regular intervals, and thoroughly spoilt! The girls were equally well looked after, and I do not remember any of them turning ghastly green after injections!

I remember that convent with great affection. I used to leave the sanatorium and walk down the fire escape to the car park ready to face the weekend after all the TLC I received there!

Primary School Work

As school nurses the majority of our time was spent in the primary schools. Although we were just guests in the schools, most of us, as the allocated nurses, felt like staff. I used to try to organise my timetable to fit in with school life and keep as regular a routine as was possible. Because of this the school knew when to expect me and were very welcoming. Nearly always I arrived in time to have a coffee and chat with the staff before school started. It gave them an opportunity to express any concerns they might have about children in their classes and also give me the opportunity to get to know them. I found, too, it was very important to make friends with the school secretary. She was the 'fount of all knowledge' and could be a great help; she almost always knew the parents as well as the children.

I was quickly made to feel part of school life and invited to all the plays and concerts, sports days and fetes. I tried to attend all that I could so that I became a familiar figure to the children and parents alike. Most of my schools were in the South Norwood area of London, and the local football team was Crystal Palace. I had to be sure I knew the score before going into school on Monday morning! Not that that was too much of a chore since my second son was by then already playing for their junior squad.

South Norwood is a very multicultural area, and this added great interest to my life. The children were wonderful, and they taught me about their cultures. Some things seemed hard to me. One day I saw a small Chinese girl, still in the infants' school. Her hands were raw and sore. The condition persisted, and so I thought I ought to make a home visit. I was welcomed warmly by her mother, who spoke very little English, and her grandmother was there, who spoke none. I tried to explain my reason for visiting and was getting lots of nods and "yes, yes", but I knew there was no comprehension. Fortunately an older child arrived home from senior school that spoke English and was able to be my translator.

"What is the problem?" I was asked.

I explained I was concerned about the small girl's hands.

"Oh, no problem!" I was told. "It is because she washes the dishes at night."

The older child told me the family ran a Chinese restaurant and they all worked in the evening.

"But she is so small; she should be at home in bed, not washing dishes!" I exclaimed.

The older child looked at me severely. "At home there is no one; at the restaurant we are all there. Once we are five, we work in the family business."

I was taken aback and not sure what to do except send a report to the headmaster and my supervisor.

"Please can you treat her hands with cream," I added.

"We will," the older child relayed back to me. "We thank you for your concern, and we will take care."

I went home saddened. What to us in our culture seemed abuse, to them was normal, and they were caring, loving people. In a way I was glad that I could 'pass the buck' and let my superiors deal with it. I knew from my time in Africa that sometimes cultures clash. I wanted to keep friendly with the family and also ensure the little girl's hands healed so visited from time to time. Her hands did heal, and the family knew that the school cared, so I guess a compromise was reached.

Sadly, we always had to be alert to the possibility of child abuse. The September after I started in school health I had the opportunity to study for a Diploma in School Nursing. It was a newly instigated course, and I attended Croydon College on a part time basis for the next six months. I found it very interesting, and for my dissertation I chose to look at child abuse. I was particularly interested in learning more about what might lead a parent to abuse a child. We always had to be on the alert for any signs of possible abuse when we examined children in school. Very sadly it does seem to be present in all strata of our society.

The course covered every aspect of our work, and I learned a great deal. I was introduced to Croydon's Health Education Department and found them so helpful in later months when I was able to develop this part of my work. It was good to meet other school nurses and learn from them too. Some have remained my friends. We shared some of our lectures with health visitors who were doing their certificated course, and that too was both interesting and helpful. It was quite hard to go back to 'school' myself. It had been a very long time since I had studied or taken exams. The family were very amused and teased me a lot about doing my homework alongside them!

My husband's health was deteriorating steadily, and the DVLC asked him to take another driving test. He was given a time one afternoon when I was doing routine medicals with a doctor at a primary school. We were halfway through the session when Phil phoned. He sounded very upset. He was stranded at West Wickham, having failed to pass the test, and was not even allowed to drive his car back home. Actually, it was not his car but belonged to Scripture Union.

The doctor with whom I was working was a very gracious lady. I always enjoyed working with her, and she knew a little of my circumstances. She sent me away to sort out the situation. I drove to the test centre and drove Phil home and then took a bus back to retrieve the other car. Phil was very angry and very upset. He loved driving, and to be deprived of the independence it gave him was a great blow.

Later that evening the doctor with whom I was working telephoned to see how things were. She explained to me that when she arrived home from work and shared the news with her husband, he immediately offered to take Phil into Croydon for work each morning. I was amazed at such unexpected kindness. The couple did live quite near us, and Don faithfully both took and brought Phil home from work for several years until he himself retired. We were so grateful to him and to our heavenly Father who had provided for us.

I enjoyed working in all of my schools, but South Norwood Primary was my favourite. It was housed in an old Victorian building and was probably the most multicultural school of them all.

Many of the children came from rather deprived home backgrounds. The headmaster worked tirelessly for his children, trying to give them the best start in life that he could. He inspired his staff, and there was always a happy atmosphere both in the staffroom and in the classrooms.

The 'nit nurse' image dies hard. We were not supposed to do routine head inspections, but the parents often became paranoid about head lice! I even held an evening lecture to inform the parents about head lice. As usual, those who attended were the ones who were already pretty well informed and did all the correct things to try and prevent infestation. The parents who didn't attend often spoke little or no English and came from cultures where head lice were just part of life. On one occasion I visited a home of a little Indian girl. She was in the reception class, and when I looked at her it appeared that she had grey hair! I looked closely and saw her hair was moving, totally covered in lice. I had never seen anything like it! After school I went to her home with some lotion for her mother to use. Mother and grandmother spoke no English at all. With gestures I pointed to the lice and the bottles and tried to explain. The next day I went to see if any of the health visitors in the area could speak Urdu. Eventually we did find an interpreter. It took a lot of persuading and explanations to get the mother to treat her daughter's condition. She saw no reason to do it; it was perfectly normal to her!

The staff at South Norwood knew that I was a committed Christian and often asked me to speak in assembly. Although not part of my remit, I was only too happy to take the opportunity. It was never too difficult to start with a medical point and move from there into something spiritual. The Lord always gave ideas. We looked at ears with an auroscope and then talked about listening to God. We tested eyes and talked about miracles Jesus did to make blind men see. I think I enjoyed those assemblies as much as the children!

Eye testing was a routine necessity. We detected many children who needed to wear glasses. Standing behind the child, covering one eye, then the next, I silently prayed for that little life. I knew the Lord wanted to bless these precious children.

It was at this school that I was asked to teach sex education. It was a subject that no-one wanted to teach, least of all me! However, when I thought about it I realised the Lord was giving me a unique opportunity to present to the year six children a wholesome view of sex and family life. I talked to the headmaster.

"If I can teach health through the whole term, taking one body system after another, ending up with the reproductive system, and if I can teach sex in the context of marriage, then I will do it," I told him.

"That sounds fine to me," he replied. "The class teacher will always be in the room with you to support you. Just work out your curriculum, and we will arrange it."

I drew up a teaching plan to cover the main body systems and the head wrote to the parents asking for permission for the children to attend. Only one Moslem family withdrew their two boys. The note that was sent to the head said, "I do not want my children to attend the sinful Mary Week's lessons."

I was teased for ever after about that!

The head ribbed me and said, "I always knew you were sinful!"

And I answered, "Yes, but I know where to go to be forgiven!"

Very quietly he looked at me and replied, "Yes, I know you do."

Preparing those lessons was great fun. The Health Education Dept. helped me enormously with visual aids. I was given a whole afternoon each week. I divided the time into two parts: in the first we learned the theory and in the second we had some sort of practical activity. When we learned about our muscles we followed it up with an aerobics session which I had devised to the 'Match of the Day' tune. After learning about respiration we used a 'smoking machine' to see how much tar was deposited from just one cigarette. The boys' favourite was after learning about circulation cutting up ox hearts! One of the boys' fathers was a butcher and donated the hearts to us. (He also gave us an ox's eye to look at when we talked about vision!) We carefully dissected the hearts, much to the girls' horror and the boys' delight. We had huge fun together. Usually I also made a word search puzzle or a quiz sheet for the children to take home, and they also made folders with health promotion leaflets.

At the end of the term when we came to talk about reproduction, there were no giggles or embarrassment because we talked about this system just like any other. For our practical session we had a mum of one of the children in the class come and bath her newborn baby. That was fine. We also had one extra lesson when the boys went with the headmaster and he talked with them about growing up while the girls came with me and talked about the changes that would happen to them as they reached puberty.

The programme was so successful that I was asked to do it each year. I was glad to help in this way, and even when our remit was changed and teaching in this way was no longer allowed on my schedule, a letter from the head to the director of school health meant the rules were waived and I could continue. After I had left the school nursing service I used my day off each week for a couple of years to continue the programme.

I had a lot of Roman Catholic schools on my patch. I don't think there was a particularly large Catholic population in the area; it seemed rather more by accident than planning. The schools were well favoured by parents, of all faiths and none, because of the good discipline and caring attitudes. One summer term I had reason to be very impressed by St Thomas a Beckett Primary School. A large group of Irish 'travellers' suddenly arrived and parked illegally on a local recreation area. There was a huge hue and cry by people in the neighbourhood. Nobody wanted to have the travellers living near them. They were really treated as outcasts. Some of them did manifest very antisocial behaviour.

The headmaster of the school sent the priest round to say that the children would be welcomed at his school for the duration of their stay. Not all the parents were pleased! The children did come to school for the few weeks before the council moved them on, and they were helped as much as possible during their short stay. They had health checks and immunisations, school dinners and uniforms provided, as well as the best education as could be given in that short while. Most of all, they were treated with respect and made to feel wanted. How terrible it must be to have people hate you wherever you go and try to get rid of you as soon as possible. Those children were just like any other children, needing love and care and to know they were loved by the Lord.

Changes Afoot!

As I have mentioned, part of my work was to help the health visitors in their baby clinics. Most school nurses resented this and felt it was not relevant to their work. I enjoyed the clinics. They were very different from our clinic at Rethy! Often the clinics were held in church halls, and all our equipment was stacked away in some cupboard. It always took a while to set up the clinic, putting out toys for the little ones to play with as well as the equipment for medical checks and immunisations. In most clinics baby food was available for sale and collection by the mothers on welfare benefits. I suppose the rationale behind school nurses helping at these clinics was that the toddlers would get to know us in the preschool years and not be afraid when they did enter school. However, it seemed more about helping some very busy and stressed health visitors who had such heavy case loads!

Because it was known that I didn't object to helping at clinics I would often be asked to go outside of our area and also from time to time asked to help during the school holidays. It gave me the opportunity to get to know the health visitors, and several of them became good friends. One of them eventually went to Kenya with the AIM mission with whom we had served. I thought their work was both important and interesting and found myself wondering if I should go to college and train to be one.

I did go as far as applying. I was awarded a place at Epsom College. However, I needed sponsorship from a local authority, and Croydon were not able to give me a grant. Lewisham did agree to sponsor me, but it meant that after qualifying I would have to work in that area. With Phil's health constantly deteriorating I felt Lewisham was just too far away for me to travel each day for work so I put the health visiting 'on hold' for a while.

I was beginning to feel that I needed a bit more challenge in my work. I had spent about four years school nursing. One of the health visitors in our office was on the committee of the Health Visitors Association, to whom school nurses were allied as a professional body. They were looking for someone to represent the school nurses on the Trades Union Council. She asked if my name could be put forward, and I agreed. The TUC accepted me for that post, but it was only for a short while as my situation soon changed dramatically.

My husband's illness, and occasionally those of the children or me, necessitated frequent trips to visit our family doctor, John Roche. He had become a real friend to us all ever since our move to Croydon and supported us through many 'ups and downs' in our health. Very often, when I was at the surgery, for some reason he would jokingly tell me that I was in the wrong job - I should be working for him! He knew that both his receptionist and practice manager wanted to retire, and he was very concerned about getting replacements. As a single handed GP, he needed to depend a great deal on his ancillary staff.

After a while, I realised that John's joking attitude was masking a serious suggestion. Yet I didn't seriously consider it. It would mean a whole change in our family lifestyle. I would not be nursing or have hours that fitted so well with family life. I had no secretarial or management skills. However John's comments just kept niggling away in my mind.

One morning I needed to take one of my children to the surgery. I had to delay going into work and had a little time before we had our appointment so used that time to pray in a very specific way. I asked the Lord, if he was speaking to me through John then could the invitation to work in the surgery be given again. After the usual wait we were called in to the doctor. We sat down, and he greeted us. Then before he asked why we had come he addressed me.

"Mary, I really believe you should come and work for me!"

I was quite taken aback at so direct an answer to my prayer.

"Can I come and see you and talk it over?" I replied.

"How about this lunchtime?" he answered.

Sometimes in my lunch break I would have a meeting with him concerning the health of children who were under the care of both of us so he knew that it was possible. Then he asked what problem Paul or Jenny had; I can't remember who was with me on that occasion.

I returned to the office quite bemused. At lunchtime I took my sandwiches to the surgery and had a long discussion with John. Every argument I put forward he seemed to have a positive answer for:

Wages?

Yes, I was on a sister's salary, but he would equal it, making sure I was earning as much.

Hours?

He would be flexible.

Inability to type well or do PAYE for salaries?

No problem; he would help me to learn! He knew that I was also on the waiting list for some fairly major surgery. He said he would get someone to cover that sick leave.

Normally I would deliberate for a long time on such a major event as changing a job. I am not given to hasty decisions, and yet for some reason I was totally sure I should say "yes" to John and did so! I returned to the office and handed in a month's notice. Everyone was shell-shocked and counselled me not to leave nursing. It seemed ridiculous to my colleagues to leave a good nursing post to become a humble receptionist and practice manager. They did not understand. I am not sure that I did either, but I felt so strongly that God was leading me. It was his golden thread being woven once again through the fabric of my life.

When this happened, Phil was not at home. He had gone to Derby with his line manager to do a stock take of a shop there and was away a few days. When he returned, I had to quietly tell him what I had done! It was not my custom to make unilateral decisions. However, God had prepared the way, and Phil was just slightly amused that his quiet little wife had made a career change while he was counting books in Derby! He, too, was absolutely sure that God was in this move.

For the next month, while I worked out my notice for school health, I set the alarm clock to wake me at 5.00am each day. After spending some time reading my Bible and in prayer, as was my custom, I then got out Phil's typewriter and with the help of a Pitman book I began to teach myself to type. Because of what I had learnt years ago in Kampala, I was at least familiar with the keyboard.

Then at work both in the office and in my schools I needed to make sure all my paperwork was up-to-date so often had to work late. It was quite a month! However, I persevered and felt a little more prepared to face the challenges of a new career in the doctor's surgery. I was very overwhelmed by the farewells which my schools and colleagues gave me. It was the end of a very happy few years in school health.

5

A New Job

Receptionist / Practice Manager

I will never forget my first day at the surgery, and I doubt if John ever forgot it either! Although I had spent a couple of Saturday mornings familiarising myself with the geography and the protocols of the surgery, it was very different suddenly being alone and in charge of an office. It's never good to start on a Monday morning in a doctor's surgery because the telephone rings incessantly for the first couple of hours. It seems as if everything goes wrong at the weekends and half the practice list insists they must see the doctor at once! While I tried to answer all the queries, see to the patients who arrived for their appointments, process repeat prescriptions, fend off the medical reps, I was becoming more and more frazzled by the minute! No wonder the previous manager had wanted to retire! I wondered if I had made a big mistake. Yet deep inside I felt the peace of God which does 'pass all understanding'. How could I feel that with all the chaos around me? Somehow I did, and that is the miracle of God's grace.

By some miracle too, by the time the district nurse arrived at the end of the morning to see her patients and John had seen all his appointments and was ready to do home visits, I was able to make a cup of coffee and tidy up the office. I was due to have a break between lunch and the afternoon surgery, which began at 4pm, but John had left a letter for me to type.

The surgery typewriter was an electric model, quite different from the one on which I had practised. It took me ages to even see how it worked! I don't know how many times I tied to type that letter ready for John to sign, but the wastepaper basket was quite full with torn up copies! I was almost in tears. I didn't leave the surgery all afternoon and only finished the letter at the end of evening surgery. I am sure he must have taken it home in despair to his wife, who was a fantastic secretary, and had her make a decent copy to send off! John was very patient with me and never complained at my slowness or mistakes through those first weeks. He was always the perfect gentleman both to his patients and to his staff. Occasionally he became irritated, but I never saw him lose his temper.

Learning the ropes in the surgery was a revelation to me. I had no idea how much paperwork was involved. All the immunisations, cervical smears, antenatal and postnatal visits, baby clinic attendances and many other such things had to be carefully recorded for the health authority. The doctor's salary was made up of reimbursement of fees so it was very important to get it right. Every three months, all the prescription which had been written and dispensed were sent back to the surgery and had to be checked through. Also there were private medicals which were done for insurance premiums and claims, and these usually happened in the afternoons after visits but always entailed long and detailed reports which taxed my typing skills. John's handwriting also taxed me! The reputation that doctors' writing was undecipherable was almost proved true. John had a habit of writing on old envelopes or scrap paper, and his writing became smaller and smaller as the letter progressed. At least my medical knowledge helped me to decipher what he was trying to write!

The end of the month salaries had to be made up and the insurance stamps purchased; this was another task which I did not find easy. That was nothing, though, compared to the nightmare that preparing the accounts for the auditor proved to be! Maths was never my strong point, and I laboured and prayed over those figures so much. With John's consent a dear friend at church who was an accountant went through the figures with me before they were presented, and that was such a help.

As soon as I began work in the surgery the previous manager/receptionist retired, but the other part time receptionist remained for a short while. She was quite elderly and also wanting to retire so John asked me if I knew anyone who might be suitable to help. As I thought and prayed about this I kept thinking of a lady whom I had been asked to visit while I was a school nurse. Although she wasn't a mother of a child in any of the schools on my 'patch', her circumstances were so similar to mine that it was thought that I might be the best person to do a home visit. In fact, her children were at same primary school as my daughter so we immediately had a link. Her husband had a disease very similar to Phil's, and the mother was experiencing reactionary problems with her eldest son. I could identify with that too as Mark had gone through a period when he struggled to come to terms with his dad's illness.

When I went to visit Julie, I found that we had even more in common for she and her husband were Christians. What began as a formal home visit later developed into friendship between our two families. However, at that first visit as I left, Julie commented to me that at least I had the security of a profession. She had married young and had not worked outside the home and wondered how she would cope if she ever needed to support the family.

I suggested to John that perhaps Julie could be our part time receptionist if she were interested in the job. He was happy for me to make enquiries so I went to talk it over with her. In a few days she phoned to say she was interested and not long after that she joined our team and was a great asset. She very quickly 'learned the ropes' and had such a kind manner with the patients that they soon grew to love her. She rarely became flustered, and her placid attitude was a blessing to the surgery.

As the three of us were all Christians, we decided to have a little time of prayer on Tuesdays, the day when Julie was working. I came down early before I took over for the evening surgery, and we spent time asking the Lord to bless our patients and give John wisdom in diagnosis.

The work was a lot for one doctor to manage. When he went on holiday we had to import a locum. Our patients didn't like this very much! Blood pressures all went up as people were apprehensive at seeing someone they did not know! John felt that perhaps he needed some help and advertised for a part time female assistant. He thought it would be good for the women to have a female doctor and wanted someone who was interested in obstetrics, gynaecology, and child welfare. So it was that Dr. Naomi joined the practice. She was a radiant Christian so our prayer meeting became a group of four. The Lord began to answer our prayers in ways far beyond our imagination. Patients began to open up and share deep spiritual needs. We found people were hungering to know God! One evening surgery is emblazoned forever on my memory, when we gave out more copies of 'Journey into Life' than we did prescriptions! We were not seeking to intrude into patients' spiritual lives, but they were asking us for help.

My church realised that God was doing something very special, and I was often asked to pray with people in need. They generously decided to pay for me to go to a CWR Introduction to Counselling course, which eventually led to accreditation as a Christian counsellor. The practice was in the area of our church so many patients who wanted to be referred to a church were introduced to ours.

One area which presented where women needed help was crisis pregnancy counselling. It seemed there were so many girls who became pregnant and didn't have anyone to whom to turn. They didn't really want an abortion but felt there was no other option. Naomi had a vision to help these women. She decided to start a Christian group that would both counsel those with a crisis pregnancy and also run a contraceptive service. So 'Nissi' was born. 'Nissi' means 'The Lord our banner' and we designed a logo with a banner on which this word was written. Then several leaflets were prepared and a prayer group set up to support the work. From a very small beginning the project grew - so much so that eventually Naomi left the practice and worked full time at Nissi.

Yet more Changes!

When I worked in Addiscombe and South Norwood as the school nurse I came to know lots of young families. Since changing jobs and joining the surgery, I found I was getting to know many older people too. I really enjoyed that. It is hard in the London suburbs to make community 'work' as so many people are commuting each day. Also the area lacked affordable housing for young couples so it was rare to have extended families in the locality. Many people led quite isolated lives and coming into the surgery would often welcome a chat. If I met them at the shops they would want to stop and talk. It might often be about their medical problem, but I realised they needed to talk. Some of the older folk in the road where I lived were very grateful if I collected their prescriptions for them.

Sometimes I would be asked about a minor health problem but occasionally a major one. One bank holiday my neighbour called me. His father had come for a visit from Australia and was doing some weeding in the garden when he collapsed. I tried to resuscitate him for twenty minutes while we waited for the ambulance, but I knew that it was in vain. I felt so sad for the family because the holiday had turned into a disaster for them all.

On another occasion a patient, who was a dear friend of ours and whose husband was a deacon at the church which we attended, phoned on a Saturday. She had phoned the surgery and in her distress could not get the out-of-hours doctor's number down correctly, so she phoned me. When she told me her husband's symptoms I immediately called 999 for an ambulance and rushed to her house. Again it was a heart attack, and I tried to resuscitate. Fortunately the ambulance responded quickly and was able to revive her husband. I followed the ambulance to the Mayday Hospital to be with my friend. Her only daughter was visiting a friend in Bath, and because we had family and contacts there while I was at the hospital, Phil was able to make contact with Heather and her husband and tell them the news. Her father died that afternoon in the hospital. I stayed there with his wife until the family arrived. Sad though it was I was so glad to be available to comfort my friend in those dark hours. After that, each Thursday afternoon I went to her for an hour before I returned to the surgery. Those hours became very precious times of fellowship for us both.

England was hit in October 1987 by the great storm - the hurricane that was unpredicted! I remember waking that morning and was amazed that all our family had slept through it. My eyes could hardly believe the devastation that I saw outside. The radio was warning us to stay indoors, but I felt a huge responsibility for my patients. Someone had to open up the surgery. I doubted that John would be able to get in as he lived some miles away in the village of Godstone. It took me a long time to walk the half mile to the surgery. I was almost blown over several times and was horrified to see how many trees had been blown down. The tarmac was ripped up on the pavements and their roots exposed. It was an awful sight! Eventually I managed to get to the shelter of the surgery, and to my amazement John was there! We opened up as usual but not one patient arrived. Their ailments must have seemed minor compared to braving the storm. At least we both caught up on paperwork and at midday decided to close up and go home. I didn't have to battle through the storm again, for John drove me home.

As John lived so far from the surgery, I was the main key holder. This meant, should the burglar alarm be activated, I was the first person whom the police tried to contact. We did have a few attempted, and one successful, 'break in' while I worked there. The surgery was in a Victorian terraced house and a fairly 'soft' target as it had old-fashioned sash windows. One night the police woke me in the early hours of the morning and asked me to go to the surgery as the alarm had been activated. They arranged to be outside the building to meet me there. The phone had woken the whole household, and Paul volunteered to drive me down. He wasn't keen on his mother driving around Addiscombe at that time of the night. I was so glad he was with me because as soon as I arrived the police cleared off! Paul and I entered the building and switched off the alarm, no doubt to the relief of all the near neighbours. I was quite nervous, having expected the police to at least look around the premises, but no-one was inside. The upstairs back bedroom window had been smashed, but little else was disturbed. Drugs were not kept on the premises, and I guess that was the reason for the burglary. I made a mental note that should the police ever call me again only agree to go down and unlock if they agree to accompany me inside! It was fortunate that Paul was still living at home; Mark was now away at university.

The following day the police came to visit, this time to investigate the scene of the crime. They found imprints of trainers in the back garden but never to my knowledge apprehended any suspect. Perhaps the alarm disturbed the person; the surgery was all in good order.

I thoroughly enjoyed working in the surgery, especially once my typing skills had improved as well as my ability to read John's writing. It was quite a steep learning curve just to be able to do that! I settled into quite a comfortable rut. The family were now well into their teenage years and didn't need me around in quite the same way as when they were young. They also helped me with Phil's care, which was increasing as the years went by. When each one reached seventeen and was eligible to get a provisional driving licence, the friends from the Missionary Mart, where Phil had helped so many years ago, gave money for them to have driving lessons. It helped me so much when the boys, and later Jenny, were able to help with transport.

I particularly enjoyed the evening surgery time. It was much quieter than the mornings when the phone constantly rang and various people called in to see John. Once I had prepared all the notes for the morning surgery and finished writing any referral letters, I usually found some time to write. I had been approached by an organisation called 'The Band of Hope' and been asked to write monthly articles for magazines they produced for teenagers and primary school children. They were to address the issues of alcohol, drug and substance abuse, as well as any other health education topics that might be relevant. Although originally a temperance society, the organisation had broadened and wanted to tackle these subjects from a Christian point of view. A short time before this request I had given up my health education teaching at South Norwood School so was very pleased to have a new interest. I really enjoyed writing for them and also a few small articles for 'Family' magazine. I really didn't mind how late the evening surgery finished because I loved this quiet time in the office. We rarely closed on time; it was quite usual to be an hour late. Writing stopped me from being frustrated or bored.

One morning I was rudely shaken out of my comfortable rut! Just before we opened the doors to start admitting patients, John called me into his consulting room.

"Mary," he asked, "have you ever considered what you will do when I retire?"

I looked at him blankly. I didn't know his exact age but had no idea he was anywhere near retirement.

"Surely you are not due to retire?" I questioned. "I haven't ever thought of working anywhere else. It's been years since I left nursing."

He could tell I was a bit taken aback by his sudden question.

"I am thinking of taking early retirement. Since Naomi left, the workload has been too heavy, and my wife's health is not good. I wanted you to be the first to know my thoughts."

It was hard to concentrate on the morning's work. What would I do? I so loved being part of a general practice, meeting so many people in the community and working in such a close-knit team. I took John's coffee to him at the end of his list, when he had a break before seeing drug firm representatives, the district nurse or going out to do home visits; he asked me to stay and he explained further.

"I have to give three months' notice to the Primary Health Care Trust so no change is imminent," he said. "However, I need to start to set things in motion now. At this stage we will not say anything to patients for they will get anxious. We will tell them when the future is settled. I have already decided that whoever buys this practice must be willing to employ both you and Julie, if you want to continue."

I knew that things would not be the same once John had retired. I also was aware that my options were limited because of Phil's progressive illness.

"At this point I can't think," I told John. "You have dropped such a bombshell!"

"I'm sorry," he apologised, "but I am sure this is the way the Lord is leading me, and I know he will take care of you, but I will do everything I can to help in any way I am able."

Over the next few weeks I felt as if I had been told I had a terminal illness, and Julie felt the same. It was worse for her in as much as this had been her first real employment and she was so enjoying it. John was as good as his word and kept us informed of any progress. One doctor who was looking for a practice came to visit, and both Julie and I took an instant dislike to him. His manner was extremely abrupt, and it felt as if he 'looked down' on us women. He was from an ethnic minority, and his spoken English was not particularly easy to understand; I knew the patients would struggle with that. We were so thankful when John told us that he wasn't going to buy the practice. When it was explained to him that buying the practice was on condition that the staff were still employed, he withdrew his application.

Not long after this John told me that the surgery a little further down the road were wanting to take us over. It meant that we would all move to their premises and they would employ an extra doctor. They had plenty of space and were willing to agree to John's terms concerning keeping Julie and I on the staff. There was only one hitch: they already had a practice manager. They couldn't dismiss her in order to employ me.

"Would you be willing to go and talk with the senior partner about options?" John asked me. "I will not let them have the surgery unless you are happily settled."

I felt very humbled that John cared so much. My mind was in turmoil, but I agreed to go and talk with the doctor as soon as could be arranged. For all of our sakes we needed to get things settled as soon as possible.

The Move

I prayed for a lot for guidance over those weeks. I felt very unsettled and concerned about my future. The Lord had made it so clear when I left school nursing and moved to John's surgery, and working there had been a spiritual oasis. I knew that nowhere else would be like that. I really didn't want to just be a receptionist; I needed the extra challenge that being practice manager had brought. Therefore it was with some apprehension that I went to talk to the senior partner at the practice which wanted to buy out ours. I didn't want to be the 'fly in the ointment' as far as the negotiations were concerned.

I was greeted warmly by a young doctor who, when we chatted, I found had trained at UCH too. He was interested to learn about my life and career so far, and when he learnt about the missionary years he told me that he was a committed Christian too. Then he put his plan to me.

"Mary," he said, "if we join the two practices together, it will mean that we have enough patients to employ our own practice nurse. Would you be willing to take on this role?"

I hesitated for a few moments. It was many years since I had been involved in hands on clinical work. I explained this to him.

"We will train you. There is a new course at Croydon College for Practice Nursing. It is a developing area of nursing in line with the government's policy of expansion of the role of general practitioners," he replied. "I have every confidence that you will manage well in the post. It will be a Sister's post with London weighting; you will not lose out on salary."

"Then I am willing to give it a try," I replied, rather hesitantly. I knew that John had told him of my family circumstances. "But I can only work part time."

"That is no problem," the doctor answered. "It will take a while for the work to build up. You can organise the treatment room as you like. It will be your department completely, but my colleagues and I will always be around to help."

I went home with my head reeling. I was so full of praise to the Lord who had gone ahead of me and provided me with a wonderful new job.

By the time I arrived back at the surgery that evening John had already heard the news. I think that I must have looked excited; I certainly felt it! I told him all about the practice nursing opportunity but also how concerned I was that I had not done any clinical work for years.

"Don't worry," he reassured me. "In these next couple of months I will teach you to syringe ears and take blood samples. I will ask the district nurse to let you take out stitches and clips and do dressings. You will soon be confident. I am so pleased for you and am sure this is a good career move."

Then he looked at me over his half-rimmed glasses and smiled.

"You would eventually have become bored being my receptionist and manager. You need another challenge!"

Over the next weeks life became very busy. All our records needed to be in order and the accounts ready for the merger. Julie and I both worked on these, and we were both so pleased that we would continue to work together albeit in different roles.

I already knew the local district nurse quite well as she visited our surgery at least twice a week. We had always been friendly, and she was very happy to teach me about the new dressings which were available. One of the common complaints treated in GP's' surgeries is leg ulcers. She gave me a wealth of advice on the best treatments, which became very valuable to me. She also allowed me to remove stitches and clips from wounds. It was so long since I had done this, but a skill well learnt, like riding a bicycle, soon returns. The patients were a little bemused to see their receptionist suddenly turn into their nurse! Many of them did not know that I had that training.

John was equally kind and allowed me to syringe ears. This was a completely new skill, as in my training it was something we were not taught. Once I had mastered that he supervised me taking blood from patients. I had been used to doing this when I was a midwife, and also in the Congo, but needed to practise. By the time we had to pack up and move I was feeling much more confident about my new role.

While all this was happening I was trying to collect donations from the patients for a retirement present for John and get a large card signed. He had a habit of wandering into the waiting room, and it was hard to keep it hidden from him, under the pile of ancient magazines that always seem to collect in surgeries! I was also arranging a surprise party for him and his wife, Myrtle, at our house. We were able to contact past and present staff and their spouses. It really *was* a surprise for John was very humble and did not expect such a send off. For Julie and me it was a joy to honour and thank someone who had been such a wonderful and kind employer.

The actual move was fairly painless. All the patients' notes were bundled up and taken down the road. Then we had to clear the surgery of fittings and furniture. It was quite sad really. Some equipment was old, having belonged to John's father who had also been a GP. Saying goodbye and moving on is never easy.

It wasn't easy for the surgery with whom we were merging either. There were several patients who couldn't see why their doctor wanted to retire, especially before he was sixty five! Change is not easy, particularly for the older patients. They were very apprehensive about seeing a new doctor.

Then the staff had to put up with Julie and I being 'part and parcel' of the deal. Julie, being the sweet and gentle soul that she is, soon fitted in. I was another cup of tea. Now they had to welcome not just me but a whole new department starting up in the treatment room. This meant separate appointments for patients who came to see me. Another doctor also joined the practice to look after the extra load of patients so it meant even more work for the ancillary staff.

Once we had all moved in and settled down together, our fears and anxieties allayed, we became good friends. So a new phase of my life began.

6

Practice Nursing

Addiscombe Surgery

*I*t was great fun setting up my own department in a brand new treatment room which had been carefully purpose-built. The first month in any new job is always challenging, and this was no exception. In my first week I went sick with food poisoning. I felt so bad at letting the surgery down. I had needed very little sick leave in my past two posts; I didn't want my new employers to think I was a person who would take 'sickies'! Then there was a much larger number of staff to get to know, and I am slow at learning names. However, they were friendly, and soon we developed good working relationships. It was the same with patients. John's patients were very pleased to see a familiar face and smiled and waved when they saw me, but it took a while to begin to get to know the other patients in the practice. I even had to get used to wearing a uniform again; I had not worn one since I was in the Congo. Neither had I used an autoclave since then. The one we had at Rethy was very old and somewhat like a living monster which had to be treated with great respect; it hissed and growled at you as if ready to explode if you didn't! Now I had to learn to use a state of the art electric autoclave. It was the first job in the morning to sterilize instruments and the last job before going off duty.

I had a clinic each day for the regular patients who had appointments for dressings, blood tests, ear syringing and other treatments. Of course, there were always extra patients who needed to be fitted in as well because they had seen the doctor and then wanted me to do something for them. Mostly this was managed without too much delay or inconvenience to other patients, but I did have one regular patient who hated waiting. He was an old customer who had plagued the district nurses for years with his bad temper and leg ulcers. These refused to heal, whatever treatment they used, and they had tried every imaginable dressing on the market. This patient was called Peter; he had developed ulcers from wounds in the Second World War and over forty years later still had them. His language was enough to make anyone's hair curl, and I think it was with great relief that the district nurses handed him into my care!

If Peter was made to wait, then he would 'let rip'. The receptionists, doctors and I would all remonstrate with him to no avail. We had to get him into the treatment room as soon as possible for the sake of everyone within earshot. He was not only an unpleasant character but also unkempt and smelly. I found myself dreading his twice-weekly visits but also praying about them.

He didn't like it very much, but I began to make him the last patient on the morning list; that way the waiting time would be reduced and not so many other patients would have to put up with his foul language. Even this solution didn't always work. One day I had to fit in an emergency appointment, and so Peter was left waiting outside the treatment room. The swearing began. I cringed every time I heard my Lord's name used in such a way. The language somehow seemed to be made worse because Peter had a speech defect, and the more his anger increased, the more pronounced this became.

When I called him into the treatment room and he began to swear at me, I felt I had taken enough. I looked at him squarely in the face and said, "Peter, you are offending me deeply because you are using the name of my Friend and Saviour in that way. If you wish me to treat you then you must stop. I will not have Jesus spoken of in that way in this room."

For a moment or two there was silence. My legs were a little wobbly; I was not used to reprimanding my patients.

"Sorry, Sister," Peter mumbled. "Sorry, I didn't mean it."

That was the beginning of a strange relationship between us. We became friends, and as the months progressed he confided in me little bits of his story. His outbursts became fewer and less violent and were always followed by an apology. He often called me 'my gal' and boasted that I had 'green fingers' for treating leg ulcers. It was a long time before they began to heal.

I used to feel nauseated when I undid his bandages - that is, if they were still in place, for Peter had a habit of removing them before he came over the road. His excuse for removing them was to say that the current treatment wasn't working. It was good when he was the last patient on the list because I had a chance to rid the treatment room of the smell that exuded from his legs.

Much later I learned why the ulcers didn't heal. He used to poke under the bandages with a knitting needle. He confessed to me that he would like his legs healed but if they were then he would have nowhere to go and no one who would talk with him!

Directly opposite the surgery was a bed and breakfast accommodation used by the council to house homeless people. Almost all the inmates were patients of the surgery and presented us with many challenges. Peter lived in a derelict caravan at the back of this property. He had lived there for years without any electricity or mains water. He cooked on a small gas camping stove.

Peter's temper got him into constant trouble; I think that had been the case most of his life. He always referred to himself as the 'black sheep' of the family, and although he had some living relatives - all professional people - he had been rejected by them. He told me once that he was a lapsed Catholic and had now pushed God out of his life. He was intelligent and well educated, with a talent for drawing. As our relationship developed, Peter would bring me pictures which he had drawn, usually on a scrap piece of paper. One Christmas I gave him a sketching pad and pencils. He was like a child when opening this small gift. He was so pleased.

Peter always wanted to say 'thank you' for the help I gave him, especially as he became more compliant and the ulcers began to heal, reducing the pain considerably. He took to helping himself to the small blue biros which were in the betting shop and bringing them over to me as a gift!

"For you, my gal," he mumbled, "'cos you have 'green fingers'."

What could I say? I guessed where they had come from for any little money Peter received from welfare benefits disappeared again very quickly 'on the horses'. I didn't want to reject him and his gift, but if I took them back to the shop it would probably make things worse. I chickened out and left them in the reception area after he had gone.

One day the long-suffering shop staff must have lost too many biros or just caught him red-handed taking them, and they called the police. A heated battle of words (and not very choice ones I am sure!) ensued, and a very disgruntled Peter plodded over to the surgery seeking support for his case. The police must have had far worse crimes to deal with for they didn't turn up to apprehend the culprit. However, the incident upset Peter so much that he went to his caravan and took every pill he could lay his hands on. Fortunately he didn't have too many around, but he did make himself quite ill. He was taken to the Mayday Hospital and underwent the indignity of a stomach washout, then was admitted to a ward. As soon as he began to recover he discharged himself by simply absconding. He turned up outside my treatment room with a needle strapped into his vein, demanding its removal! I wanted him to see the doctor, but there was no way he would agree to that. He was sure that if he did, he might end up being committed into the local psychiatric hospital and never be allowed out. Poor Peter; he was so rejected and frightened, yet so angry with the world which had treated him so badly.

It took about two weeks after this episode to restore his confidence in us before he would come again for dressings. How often I prayed for him that he would allow God's love to shine into his life!

One morning Peter arrived with a picture of a cat which he had drawn for me. My treatment room now was adorned with all sorts of his sketches, and often they were of animals. This one was not so good as usual, and he explained it was because his hands were hurting a great deal. He did seem to be less well than usual and agreed to allow his GP to look at him. He seemed very anaemic, and since he could not take care of himself, he very reluctantly went to hospital again. His blood count was extremely low. I pity the poor person who had to take his blood! Peter had such a phobia of needles that he probably had to be strapped to the bed and everyone around would have needed ear plugs! We were not surprised to learn the next day that he was back in his caravan having taken his own discharge! I went to see him and was appalled at the conditions in which he lived. I wondered if he would accept help, knowing how proud he was.

Peter had learned in conversation that my husband was a sick man. Phil had lost a lot of weight. I asked Peter if he could use any clothes that Phil could no longer wear. Much to my astonishment, Peter was delighted, and I was able to give him a variety of garments and also a new frying pan which we had been given but could not use as we had no gas in our home. The only problem was that he had no replacement shoes. He wore a size twelve, and they were hard to come by. He had requested social services to help him, but they had not found any.

One day Peter came to the surgery in an unusually bad mood. We had all become used to him being much more pleasant and compliant, but this day he was far from being so. It was his birthday, and he had just hoped that one of his rich relatives might have remembered him, even sent a cheque which might have bought his shoes, but the postman had brought nothing. He felt so rejected and angry. I had no way of comforting him but did tell him that I would pray for a pair of size twelve shoes for him.

About two weeks later Peter came in for his dressing, and he was beaming. The social services had found a pair of boots which fitted him. They had needed new soles and heels, and the local cobbler fixed them for him without charge. It was heart-warming to hear of such kindness! The amazing thing was that within another couple of weeks two more pairs of shoes had been found for him. For the first time in years Peter could choose what to put on his feet. He agreed that God did hear prayers!

The receptionists and I decided that come what may we would all send him Christmas and birthday cards and maybe even small gifts. We wanted to bring a little joy into his life. From being an unwelcome visitor to the surgery, he had become endeared to us all.

Over the time at that surgery Peter's trust in us grew and eventually I was able to not only give him his monthly injection for anaemia but even to take blood from him. His ulcers were virtually healed, yet we all knew that something was not right. He became lethargic and spent most of his time sleeping on his bunk. The years of neglect caught up on him, and just a short while before I left that post he died. He seemed to have regained some trust in God and some peace. He had even made one trip to church before he finally took to his bed. He told me it had been to pray for 'his gal with green fingers!' I was very humbled.

I learnt that for forty years he had been trying to claim some sort of military pension for the disability he had suffered as a result of the war; it was finally agreed he should receive it just before his death, but he didn't live long enough to get any money.

The Introduction of Clinics

In 1990 the government introduced a new contract for GP's. It contained a fresh emphasis on holding clinics for health promotion and education, on the premise that prevention is better than cure. In preparation for this the surgery sent me on several courses, the first of which was for the Practice Nurse Diploma. This was based at Croydon College and ran over three months with a weekly day of lectures. It was very interesting, and my dissertation was about influenza immunisation. Our surgery wanted to increase the uptake of immunisation, especially for the chronically sick and elderly patients.

I was given the job of ordering the vaccines. It was difficult to estimate how many would be needed, and I had to order them in January for the campaign which would be held the following October. The drug firm representatives were always vying with each other to try to get our order. I estimated the first year that we needed four hundred vaccines and gave my order to a firm who faithfully promised that they would be delivered during the first week of October. I arranged to book patients in after the second week in October and blocked out time to hold a special clinic for this.

The first week of October came and went – but, alas, no vaccines arrived! We were telephoning the drug company most days, and they were very sorry but could give no assurance of the vaccines arriving in time for our clinic. Our practice manager was very worried and wanted me to cancel the clinic, but that would cause such problems for the patients, many of whom were elderly and infirm. I prayed about the situation and felt sure we should just trust the Lord and prepare for the clinic. The manager was far less sure than I was but agreed to let me proceed. There were several of us in the practice who were Christians, and we prayed together. The day of the clinic arrived and still no vaccines. I had a strange peace about it all, even when the patients started to check in. Exactly half an hour before the first appointment the postman arrived with vaccine! We had one very relieved and slightly bemused practice manager, and several members of staff whose faith was strengthened! Later that day it was reported on television and radio that vaccine was scarce that year and many surgeries would not receive their quota. Not only did we receive ours on time, we were also given an extra fifty doses. What an amazing God!

We were planning to open an asthma clinic so it was suggested that I might like to do a newly developed Asthma Management course based in Stratford-upon-Avon. This was a distance learning course spread over six months with several days of study in Stratford at the beginning and the end. It was a difficult course, and I was so blessed to be able to stay with friends whom I had known in Uganda, now living at Leamington Spa. I was thrilled when I heard that I had passed the examinations, written and practical. Meanwhile in the surgery, the clinic was growing, and the doctors all supported me in my assessment and treatment of patients. I had wondered if our various proposed clinics would be welcomed by our patients. I also wondered how I would cope if they were! It almost tripled my workload, and in response to this I had a meeting with our three doctors and suggested we employed a second practice nurse. They looked at me and said, "Well, if you can find somebody, it would probably be a good idea!"

Shortly after this conversation I was out shopping in the centre of Croydon and met one of the school nurses who had been at college with me. Her family were from Goa but emigrated to Kenya and then Uganda, where she had grown up. We had got on well together on the course, and she was anxious to catch up on my news.

I told her what I was doing, and she remarked, "That sounds so interesting. I have been wondering about doing either practice nursing or occupational health nursing because I feel it is time to move on from school nursing. I like the idea of practice nursing, for my brother is a GP in South Norwood."

"Well," I answered, "if you are interested, our practice is about to advertise for someone to join me, but it will only be a part-time post."

Alba jumped at the opportunity, and shortly afterwards she was appointed and joined me in the surgery. She was a delight to work with - a very good nurse and ideal colleague. When I left she took over my role.

One of the new requirements of the government initiative was to offer all patients over seventy five years an annual health check. The patients nicknamed this their M.O.T. It was a lot of work for the ancillary staff to invite them to come but a good investment. We had a very enthusiastic response. The appointments were for twenty minutes, but we should have known better! So many elderly patients were delighted to have a chance to offload all their aches, pains and worries to the listening ear of a nurse. I remember one elderly spinster. I had asked innocently the name of her next-of-kin and then had to hear all about her family tree, especially of her niece who was a doctor in Canada. Rather a long way to come should there be an emergency!

One morning Alba was unwell so I had to take her case load as well as mine. Having managed to do all the blood tests before the van came to collect them for the hospital, I then had three 'over seventy five' checks to do. All three were very mentally alert, and I thought I had all the various questions answered and recorded and physical checks completed in a reasonable time. I thought it was a good job well done, but later that morning one of the old ladies was overheard in the Cooperative store telling another at the check-out, "You go to the surgery to see the nurse and she wants to know all about your life - nosey thing!"

The most popular clinic, particularly for the women, proved to be the weight loss clinic. We needed waiting lists to join this - I guess because it was a free version of 'Weight Watchers'. I held individual consultations, which allowed the privacy some of the clients needed. For example, one poor soul was so grossly overweight that our scales could not accommodate her bulk, and we discreetly arranged for her to go each week to visit the local butcher and get weighed on his much larger scales.

Her absolute delight when she began to gradually lose pound after pound was the greatest reward I could have asked for!

One young couple were a tonic to me. There were times when my own home situation seemed overwhelming as Phil's condition deteriorated and he needed more and more help and care. Our eldest son, Mark, was settled at university and Paul, his younger brother, had just left school and was beginning to adjust to the world of work. Jenny was doing her GCSE examinations and was unsure of her future. There were times when I just felt like getting into the car and running away for a day, screaming, "I am a person too! What about *my* needs?"

On such a day, Jane came into the surgery with her husband for a double appointment in the diet clinic. Every time that Jane and Steve attended the surgery I was humbled by their courage and inward strength. Jane was in her middle thirties and had cerebral palsy due to birth trauma. With great concentration and determination she tried to control her unruly arms and legs and produce intelligible speech. Instead of getting angry and frustrated when she could not make herself understood, she would laugh and try again. With patience and humour she wobbled around trying to take off her shoes and stand on the scales. Not only did Jane have to cope with her own handicap, but she also took care of her husband, Steve, who through a car crash became paraplegic. Somehow she managed to take care of his personal needs: washing, dressing and getting him into his wheelchair. Steve himself glowed with a real sense of wholeness and wellbeing. He was utterly proud of his remarkable wife. Their mutual respect and devotion was an inspiration to all who knew them.

In the light of their courage my feelings of self-pity just evaporated. As I discussed their new dietary regime with them, I caught their excitement because they knew it was working! With much laughter Jane eventually managed to get on the scales and record a weight loss of over a stone in just one month. She beamed from ear to ear, telling me she now could wear her 'nice' clothes again! We could not weigh Steve, but she wanted me to see how loose his trousers now were whereas previously they had been too tight to do up the button. I guessed he had probably lost about a stone too. The treatment room rang with her laughter. She would not let me help push Steve out of the surgery. She was determined to manage. All she allowed me to do was to open the door for her.

Another client who attended that clinic spasmodically was an Austrian woman, Erica. I sent her regular appointments which she rarely kept. I used to think perhaps she had given up on my advice, feeling it was pointless, when she would suddenly turn up again 'out of the blue'. I always tried to fit her in, appointment or not, because she needed help. She would 'waddle' in, placid and plump. Walking was for her a breathtaking experience these days! Erica forever stands in my memory for her beaming smile which stretched from ear to ear. A native of Vienna, she settled in Croydon many years ago but never really conquered our language. She always covered her lack of clarity with a beaming smile! Getting on the scales required a great effort, lunging first on one foot and then the other, taking several seconds to regain her balance. If her effort was rewarded by a small weight loss then I was rewarded with a huge beam. She would manoeuvre herself off the scales and flop into the chair to regain her breath.

"You gutt girl - you have chocolate," she would say and push a box of Viennese chocolates into my hands. Her sister used to regularly bring her a supply when she came over to visit.

"Now I am slim (?!) I no need," she would say in broken English.

Obviously she thought I could get fat instead of her! I felt the receptionists were needier than I, and they always gratefully received these offerings after her visits.

One day Erica arrived with her sister who had knocked her leg on a supermarket trolley and developed a leg ulcer. She too was large, and her weight problem was aggravating the ulcer. She came in week after week to have the dressing renewed, and week after week we had the same battle. Her command of English was considerably worse than her sister's and so was her understanding of the National Health System. After the leg had been dressed and bandaged neatly from knee to ankle, out would come her purse and she tried to press two pound coins into my hand. I would refuse and explain time and time again, and this charade happened twice a week until the leg healed. She could never grasp the fact that she didn't have to pay for her treatment. When she was able to return once again to her beloved Vienna, she arrived with a huge box of Viennese chocolates for me. I have never visited Austria, but it made me wonder if all Austrians are 'chocoholics' and grow exceedingly large!

Life and Death Matters

Each morning as soon as I was up I spent a while reading the Bible and trying to listen to what God was saying to me through its pages. Then I would pray, especially that I would be able to be the person God wanted me to be and show his love to everyone in the surgery. I never knew what a day would bring. I guess for me that was part of the great attraction of the job. The more time I spent talking with patients, the more aware I became of the great spiritual vacuum in which most people live.

One day I was holding my asthma clinic and a girl came in. I knew her well because not only was she a regular patient but had attended our church's Sunday School for many years, and as a young teenager she had been a member of the Covenanter class which I led. Her parents did not attend church but sent all their offspring along each week.

Normally Sally's condition was well controlled, but this time I found that all was not well. I chatted to her for a while, puzzled as to why the asthma was so problematic.

"Mary," Sally said, struggling to withhold her tears, "my life is in such a mess!"

She proceeded to tell me a very sad story which had left her very worried that she might be pregnant.

"Would you like me to do a pregnancy test for you now?" I gently asked her.

"Can you? At least then I would know for sure."

By now the tears were really flowing. Sally went off to produce the required sample. I sat and prayed for wisdom in what I said to this girl who was only the age of my own daughter.

The test was positive.

"I'll have to have an abortion; I'll have to get rid of it," she cried.

"First you need to talk to your parents, Sally," I counselled. "You are still under age, and they will have to know. You need to have some time to think before you decide what you will do next. I can give you the phone number of a group who will help you to look at every option."

I reached to the leaflets and handed her one from Nissi. I allowed her to stay in the surgery for as long as possible, and by the time she had calmed down, Sally had already decided to go home and talk to her mother. With her mother's support and that of the Nissi organisation she decided to continue with the pregnancy, and with great determination she also continued at school until just before the birth of her baby.

I was so thankful that day for the help of God's Holy Spirit so that I said things to help and not hinder this girl. I am thankful too that her baby boy's life was preserved.

Sometimes I didn't need to look at my appointment list or who was sitting on the chairs outside the treatment room to know who was coming to see me. It was always so with Mrs. Smith! She reminded me of the nursery rhyme, 'There was an old woman who lived in a shoe, who had so many children she didn't know what to do!' Mrs Smith certainly had a lot of children. Her presence in the waiting area was usually announced by her loud bellows at the small people around her skirts! She had a distinctly recognisable loud voice and normally was accompanied by all her pre-school-aged children. In the school holidays all eight would come with her; they almost needed a waiting room to themselves. How she managed to keep them all so clean and tidy with never so much as a runny nose was a mystery to me. However, remembering immunisation schedules for them all was beyond her, so whenever she did come along I tried to get all the notes for the family and catch up with any missed appointments.

When I heard her in the corridor, I prepared myself for a long session! I found that most of the other waiting patients were very tolerant, looking at her with a mixture of pity and amazement and would whisper to me, "Look after her first, dearie. We'll wait!"

She came in one day with her brood, and it was quite traumatic as one of them had caught head lice at school. She was distressed as she thought people would think her children were dirty!

"Far from it, Mrs Smith," I told her. "Head lice much prefer clean hair."

"Do they really, nurse?" she asked. "You have cheered me up 'cos I do keep 'em all clean!"

"I know you do, and they are a real credit to you," I answered as I produced lotion enough for all her family. "That means you must treat both yourself and your husband too, Mrs Smith," I told her.

I talked to the children about brushing and combing their hair, and the big girls promised to help the younger ones.

"While I am here," continued Mrs Smith, "you couldn't give me a bottle for a 'preggie' test, could you, luv? I think I may be in the family way again!"

I think I sighed as I got a bottle out of the cupboard and gave her instructions (as if she needed them) about producing the sample. Her eldest daughter gave me a cheeky grin. Mr. Smith was a long distance lorry driver, and however much we tried to help the couple, they were very erratic in their family planning method. They all lived in a small terraced house which was bursting at the seams yet spotlessly clean. The family really worked together as a unit and were also very loyal to each other. Those children had very few material possessions but were rich in love. Yes, Mrs Smith was pregnant again, and she confided to me that it really was for the last time!

Sometimes I had to deal with the sadness of young couples who could not have children. Infertility was just beginning to be treated on the NHS, but there was only one 'try'. I gave the injections to the girl, and if the attempt was unsuccessful my heart went out to them so much. Sometimes they would bankrupt themselves trying to get the money to attend a private clinic to try again. The sadness was similar when a mother miscarried a baby. Such a promise ending in nothing. Having had my own baby Alison die, I knew firsthand the pain and heartache, but I also knew my loving heavenly Father's comfort.

The one thing in life which we can be certain about is that one day, sooner or later, we will die. Working in a surgery helps you to be aware that that day can come at any time without any warning. It did for one of my patients who came for his 'over seventy five' check.

"I'm here for my M.O.T." he cheekily told me. "'Best get my certificate for another year,' I told my missus!"

The old gentleman was, as far as we were aware, in reasonably good health. He had driven his car up to the surgery and parked it outside. He had recently been diagnosed with angina, but this was not severe, and he used a spray with good effect when needed. The routine questions and tests were finished, and all that remained was to test a sample of urine.

Next to the treatment room is a toilet with a small door through which the patient is able to pass the bottle to the nurse.

I was in the treatment room and waited and waited. Finally I opened my side of the small door and asked my patient if he was alright.

"Just can't do it!" he answered. "I feel a bit 'hot and bothered', and it makes me a bit breathless," he added.

"Why don't you forget it for a few minutes, and I'll make you a cup of tea. Then you can try again, or if you prefer you can take the bottle home and bring a sample in later," I suggested.

He came out and decided to use his spray while I got a drink for him. After a few minutes he said he felt much better and would take my advice and take the bottle home. I told him to sit for as long as he needed; the waiting room was now empty.

A few minutes later I heard him call. I rushed out of the treatment room to see him sitting on the chair outside, looking ashen and complaining of severe chest pain. Fortunately two of the doctors were still in the building and helped me get the now collapsed patient onto the floor. With all the equipment we had we were only just able to keep him breathing. The emergency ambulance arrived within minutes and tried to shock the heart back into sinus rhythm. They took him to hospital, but sadly he was dead on arrival.

We were all so shocked. Here was this patient who had driven himself to the surgery for a check up, now dead - suddenly called to eternity to meet his Maker.

I had the awful job of phoning his wife to try to break the sad news. I wished I had been in a position to have driven to her and taken her myself to the hospital, but that wasn't possible. Not surprisingly, she didn't seem to be able to take in what I was saying and told me she would just put on her hat and coat and get a number twelve bus down to the hospital. I asked her first if she had a good neighbour.

"Oh yes," she said.

"Could I talk to her?" I asked.

The neighbour came to the phone, and I was able to explain a little more; she took the old lady to the hospital by taxi, and also contacted the family.

By the time I had finished doing this I was near to tears, and the receptionist fortified me with tea and biscuits. Derek, our principal GP, joined me; we were all so shocked. The other GP was a Muslim and since it was Ramadan had to abstain.

Looking back, I am so grateful to the Lord that this happened when the surgery was empty and about to close for the lunch hour. It would have been so much more difficult if we had had a waiting room full of patients.

Decisions, Decisions, Decisions!

1991 dawned. As we reviewed all that we were doing in the surgery it was perceived that there was one gap in the services which we offered. One of the doctors had a particular interest in psychiatric care and felt that we could help some of our patients by offering a stress management clinic. I was asked if I would train for this and agreed to do so. We looked at colleges where I could train, and the most appropriate was held by Dorset Health Authority.

Although the course ran for three months I was required to attend only four or five days in Bournemouth. My friend, Beryl, who had been so helpful when Phil collapsed and was taken to Mayday, was now retired and lived in a suburb of Bournemouth; she kindly accommodated me. I was so delighted to spend time with her and her brother, with whom she lived, and it made the course so much easier for me.

I think I was the one who needed the stress management! By this time my husband was not really able to continue at work. Scripture Union had been wonderful employers and had done all they could to accommodate his physical disabilities, changing his job description as needed to keep him at work. After the retirement of our friend who used to take him to work, SU paid for a taxi to enable him to still go to the shop in Croydon where his office was located. We knew that we had to make decisions about our future but were both hesitant to do so. The levels of stress in our household were pretty high! Learning about stress management was very helpful to me personally, and I believe it later proved so for many patients.

Once I had my diploma we set up the clinic. I was surprised at the good uptake. I ran it as a group session which took place over a period of several weeks. Sometimes clients requested a one-to-one session, and this was helpful to them and me to evaluate progress. The first group were almost all people who recognised that they became stressed and needed help. Once we recognise a need, it is easier to address it. Occasionally the doctors would refer patients unable to see their need, and that was a much more difficult situation.

One very good thing about this course was that our local health education provided us with leaflets, and among these was one that suggested not only looking at physical and emotional needs but also spiritual needs. Exploring this made it possible at times to share my faith without being unprofessional.

One man was sent to me by our Muslim doctor. When I talked with him he described how he felt in great detail.

"I feel all the time as if I have a big burden on my back. It weighs me down and life hasn't any joy," he told me.

I. was silent for a minute. He was describing Pilgrim in 'Pilgrim's Progress' so accurately that I felt I must talk to him about the book. I knew I would have to be very careful so I just asked the patient if he had ever read the book.

"No," he answered. "What has that to do with how I feel?"

He looked very troubled.

"If you can get that book from the library, you will find the chief character has exactly the same feelings as you are experiencing. It also tells how he found an answer! The English is old-fashioned, so you may have to persevere a bit," I added.

"Don't worry about that or the library," he told me. "If you recommend I read it then I will buy it!"

A week or so later I was confronted by the doctor who had referred the patient.

"Remember Mr. P?" he asked.

"Yes," I answered, expecting to be reprimanded for my prescription for him.

"Well, he says you told him to read a book, and he wants you to know that it has helped him so much. He will come and tell you himself soon. I think he has another appointment with you. Well done! I didn't know what to do with him. Maybe I should read it too."

"It's a great classic," I said, "with so much truth within it. It is a parable of the Christian faith."

Among all the interesting days at work were many very routine days, but because people are so interesting, they were never boring. There were times of regret too, when I missed an opportunity to be a faithful witness to Jesus. At one time I had a patient who needed regular blood tests to monitor her condition. These were very painful for her because she had veins that were impossible to see or feel, and it was very difficult to get a sample of her blood. They had so many problems at the hospital where she was treated that she asked if her GP's surgery could try.

When she came to me I was very worried, but in chatting to her in order to help her relax, I found out that she was a Christian. I asked her if we could pray about finding a vein. After all, the Lord who created her knew exactly where each vein was. She was more than happy for that so we prayed together, and then I tried and succeeded in finding a vein. Tears of thankfulness poured down her face. It had been years since anyone had found a vein at the first attempt. As she continued to come month by month, the Lord graciously helped me to reach a vein each time. Then one month I had a visiting student nurse on a learning assignment with me, and I thought it inappropriate to pray out loud with this patient. I could not get into her veins after several attempts so abandoned the procedure until another day. Afterwards I felt so ashamed and so sorry that I had caused my patient discomfort, all because I was not bold enough to pray with her in public before I inserted the needle. I asked for forgiveness from her and the Lord.

One day Phil made a decision that he would have to take early retirement on health grounds. It was very hard for him to come to this decision, but his disease had progressed to such a state that he now needed to be in a wheelchair some of the time, as walking was increasingly difficult. He began to talk about returning to his home city of Bath. He had a great longing to do so, and his brother, Gordon, who still lived there, had offered to support me in caring for him.

We prayed together about moving and felt the Lord was telling us to proceed. We talked to Paul and Jenny, who were still living at home. How did they feel? Paul wanted to move into a bedsit or small flat, as he felt settled in his work in Croydon. Jenny had finished a year in the sixth form and had been accepted at Croydon College to train as a nursery nurse. She would have been able to transfer to a college at Bath but also wanted to remain in Croydon where she had many friends and was active in the church youth group. We began to advertise in the church newsletter for accommodation for her. In fact, our pastor and his wife gave her a room in their house, just a road away from where we lived.

We put the house on the market, and in due course it was sold to a young man in our own church fellowship. We had made several trips to Bath and once again found the Lord had gone before us. A young family in the village of Combe Down, where Phil's brother and wife lived, had been trying to sell their house for some months because due to work they were moving to Southampton. They had asked their house group to pray as they urgently need to sell. The next day we began to look for a house and viewed theirs. It was most suitable for our needs, and we began the lengthy negotiations to buy it. They were thrilled to think that other Christians were buying it. It was near my brother-in-law and also the church we hoped to join.

Bath

It seemed as if everything was falling into place, but for me there was little joy in the prospect of moving to Bath. Of course, it is a very beautiful city and I had spent many of my growing years there, but I didn't feel ready to have my two younger children fledge the nest, let alone leave a job I loved so much and a church where I felt I belonged and was loved. Phil was excited so I tried to stifle my feelings, which is not a good idea! There was so much clearing out to be done, and he was not able to help me. The loft was completely floored and held so many things. That summer, when Mark was home from university, he and Paul helped me. Mark also helped redecorate some rooms before we sold it. How I had loved that house! It had been perfect for our family. Some of my turmoil was also due to the fact that my dear father was in the last stages of motor neurone disease. I tried to get to Scotland to see him as often as I could, but sadly, he died in the August before we moved.

Once I knew the move was going ahead, I began to think about work. Financially, I needed to continue to work but also I would need to be able care for Phil. I knew that I would choose to continue working as a Practice Nurse if possible. My sister-in-law worked as a bookkeeper for a practice in Bath. Phil and I knew the principal partner for he was a member of the church who had sent us out as missionaries to Congo, all those years previously.

I kept having a thought in my mind that I should contact him, so wrote a letter to him at his home address, telling him of our proposed move and asking him if he knew any practice in Bath that might need a part time practice nurse. I enclosed my CV. Once written I felt peace about it and so I sensed it had been the Holy Spirit guiding me.

This indeed was so, because the evening after receiving my letter, Ray phoned and said that very day, at the practice meeting it had been decided to employ another nurse, but to look for somebody who had an asthma diploma. He arrived home to find my letter and the CV. He offered me a job there and then, details to be worked out when I could get down for an interview! As it happened, there was a bit of a delay before we moved, but the practice held the post open for me.

Saying farewell to the Croydon practice, patients and the Church family was really hard, and it was very traumatic to leave Paul and Jenny behind, but we made the transition from Croydon to Bath without too many problems. When we left Woodside Baptist Church they presented us with a cheque to pay for an electric wheelchair for Phil. We shall never forget their love and generosity that would enable Phil to remain independent for a while longer.

I was able to have a few weeks after the move to settle us into our home before I started my new job. I knew that it would be different. My job description was mainly to be in charge of running clinics for patients with chronic diseases like asthma, diabetes and heart disease. I also had been trained to help people stop smoking, and we had a clinic for that too. I did a little work in the treatment room which included a travel immunisation clinic. Having been 'queen bee', I now needed to adjust as a 'worker' in a team of five. All the nurses in the team were very helpful and a joy to work with. Another nurse began working there on the same day as me so we both did a few days of induction together, learning the protocols which were in place. Ann was a Christian, and we soon formed a firm friendship which continues to this day.

The first day I was working alone in the treatment room I felt very insecure and like a student nurse again. One of the team came in and asked me how I was getting on, and I think my face may have said it all!

"Think of it this way," she said. "You are a fantastic cook, but it's just that you are in someone else's kitchen!"

That practical advice really helped me to adjust.

The practice was larger than the one which I had left. When I joined, four doctors worked at the place full time, plus a trainee GP. The health visitors had their own office as did the district nurses. The nurses had a treatment room plus two clinic rooms, the practice manager had her office, the secretaries another and my sister-in-law yet another. It was a happy place in which to work. Everyone had very caring attitudes towards the patients, and there was a strong Christian ethos.

Each week the practice nurses would meet one lunch hour to discuss their work and sometimes for study sessions. It was all very well structured. There were opportunities for further education and also for helping with clinical trials and research.

Demographically there were differences between the new surgery and my previous one. In Croydon, housing was so expensive that we had a very moveable population. If a young person grew up in the area they invariably were forced by economics to move to another area when they set up their own home. So we rarely had extended families in the practice. In Bath, it was not uncommon to have several generations of the same family coming to the surgery. It did bring a nice 'family' feel to the practice.

I still enjoyed health promotion and education. As one of my remits was the 'stop smoking' clinic, each year I would do a display for the National Non-Smoking Day in the foyer of the surgery. One year I was asked to talk to the children in one of the local primary schools, and afterwards the children drew pictures promoting the theme. I used them in the display, and they were very effective. I also did displays for healthy eating, asthma and heart disease prevention.

I soon began to get to know the patients who regularly attended clinics. The older clients always wanted a chat, and it was hard to keep the clinics running to time. I became increasingly aware of how lonely widowhood was for so many people. This awareness led me to start up a 'Going Solo' group later on when I too was widowed.

It had been my custom for many years to wear a 'fish' badge on my uniform. The fish was the symbol the early church used to identify them. I found that patients would also recognise the badge and sometimes ask me to pray with them. It was a privilege to do so.

Other people would ask me which fishing club I belonged to! That was also an invitation to explain to them that I was a Christian. When possible several of us who were Christians would meet together to pray for the surgery and other concerns.

One big concern which emerged at that time was that several of us were troubled by the spiritual indifference of our own children. So at that time I felt it would be supportive to start a prayer fellowship, and this ran for many years, extending beyond the group of us who worked in the practice to many of our other friends. We had a prayer letter every few months where we asked for our children to be prayed for by name. Praise God, we did have some answers to prayer. One 'prodigal' girl who was breaking her parents' hearts not only came to faith but so did her partner. They married and went for theological training and into full time Christian work. What an encouragement!

In the nursing department of the surgery we had quite a turnover of staff at one time for various reasons. This resulted in my role changing so that I no longer did any work in the treatment room. I was responsible just for the running of chronic disease management clinics. As Phil's condition worsened I had to cut the number of hours I worked. The management of the surgery were very understanding and supportive.

When Jenny had finished her training she took a job as a 'live in' nanny for a family in Limpley Stoke, just a few miles from us. It was wonderful to have her near and see her more often. It was a help to me too as she would come up and be with her father at least one evening a week in order that I could go to do the grocery shopping without rushing.

Ann, who had started working at the surgery at the same time as me, had become engaged. Her fiancé was a young man who had worked for Scripture Union in Bristol and knew Phil. It was a lovely connection. Just before she was married, we held a 'wedding shower' in our home for her. Almost all the surgery staff were able to come, and we had such a good time together. It was great too for Phil to meet all the people with whom I worked, putting faces to names. After their wedding, Ann's new husband, Andy, came from time to time to visit Phil, and it gave him great pleasure to be able to talk about times in SU. Another great friend who had been Phil's best man at our wedding also tried to come regularly, and they enjoyed playing card games together. How grateful I am to these friends, as well as to his brother, Gordon, and his cousin, Alan, who helped me so much. Without their help I would not have been able to continue working.

We had joined a small church in Combe Down village: Union Chapel. Gordon and his wife, Margaret, had belonged to this fellowship for many years. The church members were loving and supportive to us, and the pastor and his wife became very good friends.

Phil's social worker felt that he would benefit from a day each week at the Cheshire Home a few miles away at Timsbury. Our pastor felt that I should have that day as a 'day off'. Normally a taxi arrived to transport him there, but he needed someone to bring him home. Pastor Peter undertook to do this. He and Phil got on so well together. By this time speech was a problem for Phil and he had a 'light writer' machine to help. However, on one of their trips home from Timsbury, Peter and Phil discovered they could converse by singing to each other. They did this with great success thereafter.

One lunch time I went into work for an afternoon clinic. I was about to start when the district nurse popped in to talk to me about a patient. She looked at me thoughtfully.

"Mary," she said, "is everything alright at home? You look very tired."

"Yes," I answered, "everything is okay, but this morning was Phil's bath morning, and I do get tired out doing that."

Phil was quite a large man to get in and out of the bath, especially since I am 'vertically challenged'!

"There is no reason why you should be doing that," she said. "The district nurse team can help."

"I don't think he would let you!" was my reply, thinking how shy and modest Phil was.

"Well, I'll just pop in on a pretext of needing to know something next week when you bath him. That will break the ice, and I can tell him you need help. Don't worry; we have to reassure many of our patients!"

Good as her word, the following week she arrived in the middle of Phil's bath time. Once he had got over the initial embarrassment of being seen in his birthday suit in the bath, he agreed with the nurse that I was getting worn out and maybe it would help if the district nurses team helped.

It did help me, but since he needed attention four or five times a night, I was still finding I was always weary. The medical team and social worker then arranged for regular respite care, which then gave me a week every few months when I could sleep! I tried to arrange for leave on those weeks in order to get away. I found myself restless if I was at home and wanting to go to the home to visit Phil, and he was always on the lookout, hoping I would arrive. It was better if I could get right away. One time I even went to the USA to see my spiritual mum, Marcie. It was such a blessing to me, and praying with her gave me renewed strength to go on, as did my visits to our very special friends at Weymouth. These friends had been so kind to us through so many years, giving our whole family holidays when otherwise we would not have been able to have any. One help came from a most unexpected source. The nurses' league at UCH heard of Phil's illness and offered to help. So they paid for a telephone life line rental. This meant that if I was at work, Phil could always get help just by pressing the button he wore around his neck. It gave me reassurance that he was safe when I was out of the house.

Even with all the wonderful help and support, the years of care were taking their toll physically on me, and an ongoing problem of arthritic hands worsened. There were some procedures which required dexterity of movement which I was now finding increasingly difficult and painful. It all came to a sudden conclusion when I was sent to see an occupational health specialist who declared I was unfit for my job. I was totally devastated. He would not even let me see the week out. I felt bereft, bereaved even, at the loss of my job and the suddenness of it all. I was angry with the Lord. I had always sought to do my job well and give my patients the very best care I could. Now I felt as if I was suddenly thrown on the scrap heap, past my 'sell by' date!

However, I knew deep down that the Lord was in it all. His golden thread was still there because on the very day I was told I would have to leave, I received a letter from a friend. Her aged mother had died, and she and her family were not in need of all the inheritance but felt they would like to give me a gift. It was a large sum which, when my sister-in-law worked the figures out, would have been my salary for the next two years, after which I would have reached retirement age. How amazing was that!

I missed my work and especially my regular patients, but Phil now needed me at home all the time. It was the right time for me to have left. We didn't know that we had less than two years left before the Lord would call him home. It was the end of a wonderful, God-planned career.

7

All Things Must Pass

*L*ife soon settled down into a routine revolving around the nursing care which Phil needed. It is never so easy to nurse one's nearest and dearest. With patients, however well you have got to know them over the years, there is always a certain detachment, but with family there are the ties of emotional involvement. If there was one verse of scripture which the Lord kept bringing to my notice through this time it was Jeremiah chapter twenty nine and verse eleven:

"'For I know the plans I have for you,' declares the Lord, 'plans to prosper you and not to harm you, plans to give you hope and a future.'"

It was very comforting to know that all that was happening to us was allowed within the love of God and that he had good plans for our futures.

The occupational therapist was always very helpful, trying to enable Phil to remain at home. In common with so many disabled and frail people he had a great dread of being put into a home. When we had lived in South London we used to regularly pass a hospital which had engraved over the door "Hospital for Incurables". Phil hated it! He always used to comment to me, "Don't ever let me end up in there!"

Getting upstairs at night time was now almost impossible, and because of the structure of the house we had few options open to us. We had been discussing these with the OT one day and as she was leaving her parting shot was, "You could always move into a bungalow!"

The village of Combe Down has very few bungalows and rarely do they come on the housing market. Even so, the thought did resonate in my mind, and I asked the Lord to show me specifically if that was to be the way forward. I needed clear guidance. Caring day and night was exhausting, and I found often I would read a Bible passage, but my brain was too tired to take it in and prayer was equally a challenge.

The next day I went to do my shopping in a local shopping area. I noticed a pile of property papers outside the estate agent and put one in my basket. Back at home I looked through it and became quite excited when I saw there was a bungalow up for sale in a street very near Phil's brother. The price was reasonable, although it looked a little shabby. Phil and I agreed that it was worth us taking a look at it. It was a Friday evening and Gordon was away, but one of the deacons at our church was an architect, as was his wife. They lived in the village and we asked them, if we could get a viewing, would they mind coming with us?

The next morning, the four of us went to see the bungalow. I was glad that our friends were with us because I would have rejected the property on first sight, but they, being architects, could see that the building was sound and also could see the potential. By that evening, our friends had drawn up some rough plans of how we could adapt and make it suitable for the wheelchair. Phil was very enthusiastic. He could see how much easier life would be for him. I inwardly groaned at the thought of moving house again and all the work involved.

Once again, the Lord was so good to us. After the weekend we asked an estate agent to value our property with a view to selling. Then we put in an offer for the bungalow. Phil needed a prescription so I went to the surgery. (We were registered at the surgery where I had worked.) As I was leaving, one of the secretaries came up to chat, and I told her we were thinking of moving house. She became excited and begged me not to advertise the house before she had spoken to her husband. They had just decided they needed to move and wanted to be nearer their daughter, who lived a few roads away from our house. The Lord had a buyer for us! These friends came to see our house and loved it. The sale went through without any stress.

With lots of help from relatives and friends we packed up. The bungalow needed extensive alterations which could not be started until the sale was completed. Our architect friends undertook to oversee the work, for which I was so grateful. Meanwhile, our furniture went into storage and our dear Pastor Peter and his wife, Lin, took us into the manse. We lived there with them for three months. For me they were months of encouragement.

When we finally moved into our new home, on a lovely sunny August day, we were delighted. It certainly made life easier for us and gave Phil a better quality of life than he had before.

The following December there was an unexpected cold snap, and we had a significant snowfall. We were all surprised by this as it had been some years since Bath had experienced snow. There was an elderly lady living next to us whose mobility was impaired so I decided that I would go to our local parade of shops to get plenty of milk and bread for both households and also get Phil's drug supply in case the weather worsened. I was worried that our neighbour might fall if she were to venture out. So I donned my boots and anorak and braved the weather. While the chemist was making up the prescription I went to the small supermarket next door. Loaded with supplies, I slipped as I left the store. I knew instantly that I had broken a bone for the pain was so intense. The manager of the shop dialled 999 for an ambulance and the pharmacist came rushing out to see if he could help. Fortunately, as we were such regular customers, he knew who I was and a little of my situation. I asked him to phone my sister-in-law at the surgery so that she could arrange for someone to take care of Phil. Soon I was in the ambulance on my way to the Accident and Emergency Department.

My left ankle was fractured, and due to the nature of the injury I needed to be in hospital for some time. The swelling had to be reduced before surgery was possible, and that meant for me Christmas in hospital and for Phil in a care home. It was the first Christmas we had not spent together in thirty two years and was made worse by the fact that one of our twin baby granddaughters was also in a London hospital having major brain surgery to save her life. She was just three months old. On Boxing Day Gordon brought Phil over to see me, and the hospital sister managed to link us up to talk to Paul in King's College Hospital, London on the phone and hear how Danielle was after her surgery. That was a kindness I will never forget.

I was allowed home on crutches just a day or so before the millennium. It was another three months before I was fully mobile and Phil could join me. They were difficult months, not only for us but also for Paul and his family as Danielle had one crisis after another. When it was all over, Mark and his wife, Sarah, came for the weekend. They had promised to come and cook us a Christmas dinner since the turkey was still in the freezer and the pudding in the cupboard. We got up on the Sunday morning and when we went into the living room we found that after we had gone to bed they had put up a Christmas tree and lots of gifts under it. We celebrated Christmas that March! None of us had any idea that we would never celebrate it together again.

In April I woke one Sunday morning, and the sun was streaming in the bedroom window. I had a strong feeling that we should go to Croydon to see Paul and his family. I hardly dared suggest it to Phil because we normally would not miss a Sunday morning service except for sickness. However, the feeling was so strong I felt it must be from the Lord. Phil agreed, and I got him ready, phoned the family, and we drove to London. I am not a very confident driver, but this time I was content to do the return journey in one day.

We had a wonderful day with Paul, his wife, Joanne, and our granddaughter, Jade, who was then seven, and the twins, Danielle and Louise, who were seven months old. We had not seen the twins since they were born the previous September and were still in incubators in the hospital. Although Danielle had multiple problems which left her handicapped, it was such a joy to see her little smile. Phil loved cuddling them all!

How glad I was that I had listened to the inner prompting of the Holy Spirit and made that trip. Just a few short weeks later Phil collapsed at home. It seemed he had a cardiac episode, and he was taken into hospital. Once stabilised, his neurologist felt it was time to do some tests and intense physiotherapy. He was waiting some weeks for one particular test, but finally it was done. The following Friday I met with his neurologist and our surgery district nurse so that we could plan for his homecoming. The consultant really felt the time was approaching when he would need full time care in a home, but the district nurses promised to give more support and we would at least try being at home for a while. His discharge was then duly scheduled for the following Tuesday.

The family all visited that weekend. When Paul left on Saturday afternoon he bought his father a Mars Bar, his favourite treat. His eyes lit up so much when he saw that! My usual routine when Phil was in hospital was on Sunday to go to chapel first, then to look after him for the rest of the day. The neurological ward he was in had many patients who needed a lot of care with washing, dressing and feeding. I always tried to go to do as much as I could for Phil, especially being there to help him with his lunch. If he had waited until the nurses were free to help him, it would normally be cold and unpalatable.

That Sunday morning I woke about five o'clock with a start! I knew I should go to the hospital. I got ready and was there just as the day staff were coming on duty. Phil was moaning. His speech was very indistinct, but I could make out that he was saying, "Ease the belt; ease the belt."

Of course he wore no belt but was experiencing abdominal pain. Then he tried to tell me it was like renal colic. Once in the past, Phil had had renal colic due to a kidney stone. He had been in agony and had needed morphine-like drugs to keep him comfortable. I went to find the charge nurse.

"Phil is in pain," I told him.

"Yes," he replied, "I have given him some paracetamol."

"This pain is too severe for that," I answered. "He is comparing it to renal colic. He has a high pain threshold. I know he is in agony. Please get someone to see him."

The nurses knew me well as I spent so much time on the ward. The charge nurse agreed that he would send for the duty houseman to come and see Phil. Unfortunately, being a Sunday, it was a relief doctor who came, not one who was familiar with his condition. However, she examined Phil and decided to order blood tests and x-rays. These showed that Phil had an intestinal obstruction. The surgeons were called, but we all agreed that his weak condition was such that surgery was not a good option.

I telephoned all the family and stayed all day with Phil. He was conscious and asked to see Peter, our pastor friend, who by now had left

Combe Down but was still in the area. By bedtime he was comfortable, and the nurses told me to go home and sleep.

On the Monday, Rowland and Sally (Phil's older brother and wife) came up from Gloucestershire, and also Gordon and Margaret. I had called the children because he was not improving. They all came. Paul must have broken every speed limit to get down from London in the time he did, and he arrived just in time to say goodbye to his father. By this time Phil's brothers had gone, and it was the children and I who held his hands as he passed from this world to be with the Lord he had loved and served through his life.

A New Chapter Begins

Death is always a shock, however well we think we are prepared for it. For me, it was no exception. I was bewildered. Phil's care had been the focus of my day for so long. I missed his companionship and friendship, his wisdom and humour as well as all the things which had previously made up my day. Mark and Sarah also moved to live in Portugal within a month of his death. I felt 'lost' within the home which had been so carefully restructured for his use.

It took me several months to work through my grief and overcome the tiredness which had dulled my senses for years. How grateful I was for loving family and friends, who prayed for me and with me, phoned me regularly, helped me sort finances and made sure I could manage.

Sometime early in 2001 I was praying and sensed the Lord saying to me that he had a new season for my life. I accepted that and told him I was willing for him to lead me into it.

One of Phil's colleagues from Scripture Union days had been out of the country when Phil had died. On his return he contacted me with his condolences. In the course of conversation we were talking over 'old times' and I mentioned the 'three musketeers', as I had called Phil, Richard and another colleague, Robert Hicks, who had also retired to Bath. Richard had lost touch with Robert through the years and was thrilled to get news and be able to reconnect with him. Richard was a trustee for a missionary society called Signpost International, and Robert owned a successful publishing business, the profits of which went to sending scriptures around the world. As a result of the reconnection between these two men, twenty thousand gospels were sent out to the Philippines. Phil would have been thrilled! The contact with Richard also linked me with Signpost International. They were taking a road show around the country that year and had a free evening in the West Country. Richard asked if I thought that our church would be willing to host a meeting. I was the missionary secretary for the church and so was able to arrange the meeting. It was well attended and well received. A challenge was given at the end of the meeting for people to go on a team to Brazil for two weeks to encourage the work with street children. I felt moved by the challenge, particularly as I had supported a street child for the past few years, and volunteered to go.

This all happened in May 2001, but by July the situation in Brazil had changed. The local church with whom the mission worked had decided it was time to change their strategy and move the girls from one large home into family units and therefore it was not an appropriate time to send a team. I felt quite disappointed. The administrator from Signpost contacted me and asked if I would go instead on a proposed team to Rwanda the following November. I wasn't at all sure about that. It was for three weeks instead of two, would cost considerably more money, and I wasn't sure that I could cope with returning to Africa where I had so many memories of Phil.

The administrator contacted me several times. She said that in prayer times about the team, my name kept coming up. Please would I pray seriously about joining the team? I asked the Lord to clearly show me and provide the finance if I was to be part of the team.

Within twenty four hours of praying like this a dear friend rang up and asked about my trip to Brazil. I told her it wasn't happening.

"Where are you going, then?" she asked.

It was such a strange question, when I think back on it. It must have been the Holy Spirit prompting her.

"Well," I answered, "I have been asked to go to Rwanda."

"Good!" she replied. "My husband and I would like to pay your fare."

Wow! I was left in no doubt that I should go to Rwanda and rang Signpost to say so. Things seemed to move very quickly from there, with training days and injections and all the other necessary preparations.

When I had broken my ankle so unexpectedly eighteen months previously the manager of the supermarket, because I had fallen on the store's threshold, had reported the accident to the local authority who owned the precinct. The result of this had been a much unexpected visit from their accident investigator. Much to my surprise I was awarded six thousand pounds in compensation. I had recovered very well from the injury and even had the pins and plates removed. It would never have occurred to me to make a claim, but it was all done for me by the local authority. It was a wonderful provision because money was not very plentiful. It meant I could put a really nice headstone on Phil's grave and also had money for this mission trip. How wonderfully the Lord looks after us!

As soon as I stepped on Rwandese soil, I knew it was right to return to Africa. I loved being back, even in the midst of such a legacy of pain and trauma after the 1994 genocide.

The purpose of our trip was to conduct a needs assessment to see how Signpost International could best use its resources to help widows and orphans from the genocide. Some of the things we saw and stories we heard were harrowing. How much these poor people had suffered.

We came home and had a debriefing weekend where we presented our findings, but the needs of the people kept tugging at my heart. I prayed and asked the Lord what else I could do to help. He gave me the idea of making greetings cards and selling them. I really enjoyed this. It helped fill the empty days through the winter, and I was delighted at how much money I was able to raise.

One day the following May I woke up with tears streaming down my face. All that morning the tears continued. I was aware that somehow I was crying for Rwanda. Not really knowing why, I phoned the administrator at Signpost.

"I am so burdened for Rwanda," I explained. "I just can't stop crying. I don't really know why I am phoning you, but it seemed the right thing to do!"

"Maybe you should join the summer team who are going out," she suggested.

"But I know that team is already complete," I answered, for I had read that in the magazine.

"If you had phoned an hour ago, I would have told you that, but in the past hour someone has cancelled. Would you take their place?"

Isn't it amazing how God works? My tears dried up, and I agreed to go back to Rwanda. I knew he would provide for me and he did! The wife of my godfather had died at a ripe old age, having been in care for some years. I was amazed when her niece contacted me to say that she had left me a legacy. It more than covered my costs!

So I returned once again to Rwanda. I was falling in love with the country and her people. On that trip I was introduced to a pastor from Mbarara, Uganda, who asked me to visit their church. I promised to pray about it. The following year I visited both Uganda and Rwanda.

Then the Archbishop of Rwanda asked me if I would do health education among the women in the Kigali diocese, and we drew up a five year plan of teaching. It was fantastic to return and do something I so loved! As well as teaching health promotion I was asked if I would help set up a day care centre with the Mothers' Union at the Anglican Cathedral in Kigali. Heather (my flatmate from UCH 'nursery' days) and I went out to help get it started in 2003, and the following year I went to work in it for three months. In the years since then it has grown and grown and now has a nursery school attached.

I returned from that trip feeling very tired and went on a holiday with a Christian group to Crete. It was the first time I had ever had such a holiday and was a wonderful experience. While there I met a widower who had lived many years in Africa and was an Anglican minister. We struck up a friendship which eventually led to our marriage in 2006. Malcolm, in retirement, was caring for a small church in North Ockendon, Essex, so I joined him there.

The Archbishop of Rwanda had approached me, asking me to consider working with the Provincial Women's Development Officer to conduct a programme of Family Planning Awareness. The government was seriously trying to address the problem of over-population of this small country. I agreed to do my best to help and began a programme of teaching in two parishes in each diocese. This was merely scratching the surface so our next campaign was to train the Mothers' Union Presidents and Vice Presidents from each parish to become advocates for family planning. I wrote a manual which was then translated into Kinyarwanda, and we have visited each diocese to train these leaders. It proved quite a difficult task as many women have no understanding of their biology because they only had one or two years at elementary school. Once they had mastered how their own body works, they found it easier to understand that family planning does not equate to "killing babies", which has been their great fear. Gradually we have overcome ignorance, fear and prejudice. The Anglican Church has been a prime mover in this area, working with the Minister of Health of Rwanda. It is too early as yet to evaluate the effectiveness of our programme, but we pray it will have been helpful.

After my marriage to Malcolm, suddenly I had a new role: a vicar's wife! It was quite a culture shock for me. The church members, however, were most kind and welcoming, and I enjoyed being among them. I was able to continue trips to Rwanda, and Malcolm was released to join me. We also went to Burundi together for a three week mission trip with Mission International, at the end of their civil war in 2008.

Over the decade since Phil's death another door was opened for me. I had opportunities to write books. Through the years I had written a few articles, poems and hymns, and a small anthology of poems was published in 1999. Then I was asked to write three biographies and also I had great fun writing several children's stories. This new career has given me such satisfaction. All my past experiences give insights which I can use in stories. I have learned that God's golden thread runs through our lives and not only blesses us but also others. How wonderful to have a Father who plans for us in love! I would never have chosen to be a nurse, but I am so glad that he chose that path for me.

Glossary of Abbreviations

AIM	Africa Inland Mission, now Aim International
BARTS	St. Bartholomew's Hospital, London
BCMS	Bible Churchman's Missionary Society, now Crosslinks
CU	Christian Union
CMS	Church Missionary Society, now Church Mission Society
CAR	Central African Republic
CWR	Crusade for World Revival
DRC	Democratic Republic of Congo
DVLA	Driver & Vehicle Licensing Agency
D&C	Dilatation and Curettage
GP	General Practitioners
IHNCF	Inter Hospital Nurses' Christian Fellowship
MAF	Missionary Aviation Fellowship, now Mission Aviation Fellowship
MOT	Ministry of Transport
MRC	Medical Research Council
NHS	National Health Service
OH	Obstetric Hospital
OT	Occupational Therapist
PTS	Preliminary Training School
RVA	Rift Valley Academy
SRN	State Registered Nurse, now Registered Nurse
SCM	State Certified Midwife, now Registered Midwife
SU	Scripture Union
TUC	Trades Union Congress
UCH	University College Hospital, London
UFM	Unevangelised Fields Mission